Roads to Mussoorie

Ruskin Bond's *Tales and Legends from India*, *Angry River*, *The Blue Umbrella*, *A Long Walk for Bina*, *Hanuman to the Rescue* and *Strange Men, Strange Places* are also available in Rupa paperback. The *Ruskin Bond's Children's Omnibus* has been a firm favourite with young readers for several years. *Ghost Stories from the Raj*, *The Rupa Book of Great Animal Stories*, *The Rupa Book of True Tales of Mystery and Adventure*, *The Rupa Book of Ruskin Bond's Himalayan Tales*, *The Rupa Book of Great Suspense Stories*, *The Rupa Laughter Omnibus*, *The Rupa Book of Scary Stories*, *The Rupa Book of Haunted Houses*, *The Rupa Book of Travellers' Tales*, *The Rupa Book of Great Crime Stories*, *The Rupa Book of Nightmare Tales*, *The Rupa Book of Shikar Stories* and *The Rupa Book of Love Stories* are some of his anthologies for Rupa. His recent books, *The India I Love*, and *A Little Night Music* have been critically acclaimed.

Roads to Mussoorie

Ruskin Bond

Rupa . Co

Published 2005 by

Rupa & Co

7/16, Ansari Road, Daryaganj,
New Delhi 110 002

Sales Centres:

Allahabad Bangalore Chandigarh Chennai
Hyderabad Jaipur Kathmandu
Kolkata Mumbai Pune

Typeset in 13 pts. AmericanGarmound by
Nikita Overseas Pvt Ltd,
1410 Chiranjiv Tower,
43 Nehru Place,
New Delhi 110 019

Printed in India by
Gopsons Papers Ltd
A-14 Sector 60
Noida 201 301

From Bangalore to old Vellore
From Puri to Mussoorie
From Chandigarh to every ghar
New Delhi to Siliguri
From Chennai's shores to Mumbai's doors
From Kolkata to Kochi
From north to south and east to west
Those gentle people are the best
Who love their books and spend their leisure
In reading both for worth and pleasure.
To these good readers, young and old,
I pay respects as hands I fold,
And dedicate these words I pen—
And dare to hope they'll pay for them!

R.B.

Composed at Shamli, on my way to Mussoorie

Contents

Backward

Instead of a Foreword I'm writing a Backward, because that's the kind of person I've always been....Very backward. I write by hand instead of on a computer. I listen to the radio instead of watching television. I don't know how to operate a cell-phone, if that's what it's still called. Sometimes I read books upside-down, just for the hell of it. If I have to read a modern novel, I will read the last chapter first; usually that's enough. Sometimes I walk backwards. And in this book I take a backward look at people I've known, and interesting and funny things that have happened to me on the way up to the hills or down from the hills.

In fact, I urge my readers to start this book with the last chapter and then, if they haven't thrown their hands up in despair, to work their way forwards to the beginning.

For over forty years I've been living in this rather raffish hill-station, and when people ask me why, I usually say 'I forgot to go away.'

That's only partly true. I have had good times here, and bad, and the good times have predominated. There's something to be said for a place if you've been happy there, and it's nice to be able to record some of the events and people that made for fun and happy living.

I have written about my writing life and family life in *The India I Love* and other books. The stories, anecdotes and reminiscences in this book deal with the lighter side of life in the hill-station, with the emphasis on my own escapades and misadventures. Over the years, Mussoorie has changed a little, but not too much. I have changed too, but not too much. And I think I'm a better person for having spent half my life up here.

Like Mussoorie, I'm quite accessible. You can find me up at Sisters Bazaar (walking backwards), or at the Cambridge Book Depot (reading backwards), or climbing backwards over Ganesh Saili's gate to avoid the attentions of his high-spirited Labrador. You are unlikely to find me at my residence. I am seldom there. I have a secret working-place, at a haunted house on the Tehri road, and you can only find it if you keep driving in reverse. But you must look backwards too, or you might just go off the edge of the road.

I shall sign off with the upside-down name given to me by the lady who'd had one gin too many—

'Bunskin Rond'
Ledur (the village behind Landour)

ONE

Breakfast Time

I like a good sausage, I do;
It's a dish for the chosen and few.
Oh, for sausage and mash,
And of mustard a dash
And an egg nicely fried—maybe two?
At breakfast or lunch, or at dinner,
The sausage is always a winner;
If you want a good spread
Go for sausage on bread,
And forget all your vows to be slimmer.

'In Praise of the Sausage'
(Written for Victor and Maya Banerjee,
who excel at making sausage breakfasts)

There is something to be said for breakfast.

If you take an early morning walk down Landour Bazaar, you might be fortunate enough to see a very large cow standing in the foyer of a hotel, munching on a succulent cabbage or cauliflower. The owner of the hotel has a soft spot for this particular cow, and invites it in for breakfast every morning. Having had its fill, the cow—very well-behaved—backs out of the shop and makes way for paying customers.

I am not one of them. I prefer to have my breakfast at home—a fried egg, two or three buttered toasts, a bit of bacon if I'm lucky, otherwise some fish pickle from the south, followed by a cup of strong coffee—and I'm a happy man and can take the rest of the day in my stride.

I don't think I have ever written a good story without a good breakfast. There are of course, writers who do not eat before noon. Both they and their prose have a lean and hungry look. Dickens was good at describing breakfasts and dinners—especially Christmas repasts—and many of his most rounded characters were good-natured people who were fond of their food and drink—Mr Pickwick, the Cheeryble brothers, Mr Weller senior, Captain Cuttle—as opposed to the half-starved characters in the works of some other Victorian writers. And remember, Dickens had an impoverished childhood. So I took it as a compliment when a little girl came up to me the other day and said, 'Sir, you're Mr Pickwick!'

As a young man, I had a lean and hungry look. After all, I was often hungry. Now, if I look like Pickwick, I take it as an achievement.

And all those breakfasts had something to do with it.

It's not only cows and early-to-rise writers who enjoy a good breakfast. Last summer, Colonel Solomon was out taking his pet Labrador for an early morning walk near Lal Tibba when a leopard sprang out of a thicket, seized the dog and made off with it down the hillside. The dog did not even have time to yelp. Nor did the Colonel. Suffering from shock, he left Landour the next day and has yet to return.

Another leopard—this time at the other end of Mussoorie— entered the Savoy hotel at dawn, and finding nothing in the kitchen except chicken's feathers, moved on to the billiard-room and there vented its frustration on the cloth of the billiard-table, clawing it to shreds. The leopard was seen in various parts of the hotel before it made off in the direction of the Ladies' Block.

Just a hungry leopard in search of a meal. But three days later, Nandu Jauhar, the owner of the Savoy, found himself short of a lady housekeeper. Had she eloped with the laundryman, or had she become a good breakfast for the leopard? We do not know till this day.

English breakfasts, unlike continental breakfasts, are best enjoyed in India where you don't have to rush off to catch a bus or a train or get to your office in time. You can linger over your scrambled egg and marmalade on toast. What would breakfast be without some honey or marmalade? You can have an excellent English breakfast at the India International Centre, where I have spent many pleasant reflective mornings.... And

a super breakfast at the Raj Mahal Hotel in Jaipur. But some hotels give very inferior breakfasts, and I am afraid that certain Mussoorie establishments are great offenders, specializing in singed omelettes and burnt toasts.

Many people are under the erroneous impression that the days of the British Raj were synonymous with huge meals and unlimited food and drink. This may have been the case in the days of the East India Company, but was far from being so during the last decade of British rule. Those final years coincided with World War II, when food-rationing was in force. At my boarding school in Shimla, omelettes were made from powdered eggs, and the contents of the occasional sausage were very mysterious—so much so, that we called our sausages 'sweet mysteries of life!' after a popular Nelson Eddy song.

Things were not much better at home. Just porridge (no eggs!) bread and jam (no butter!), and tea with *ghur* instead of refined sugar. The *ghur* was, of course, much healthier than sugar.

Breakfasts are better now, at least for those who can afford them. The jam is better than it used to be. So is the bread. And I can enjoy a fried egg, or even two, without feeling guilty about it. But good omelettes are still hard to come by. They shouldn't be made in a hurried or slapdash manner. Some thought has to go into an omelette. And a little love too. It's like writing a book—done much better with some feeling!

TWO

On the Delhi Road

Road travel can involve delays and mishaps, but it also provides you with the freedom to stop where you like and do as you like. I have never found it boring. The seven-hour drive from Mussoorie to Delhi can become a little tiring towards the end, but as I do not drive myself, I can sit back and enjoy everything that the journey has to offer.

I have been to Delhi five times in the last six months—something of a record for me—and on every occasion I have travelled by road. I like looking at the countryside, the passing scene, the people along the road, and this is something I don't see any more from trains; those thick windows of frosted glass effectively cut me off from the world outside.

On my last trip we had to leave the main highway because of a disturbance near Meerut. Instead we had to drive through about a dozen villages in the prosperous sugarcane belt that dominates this area. It was a wonderful contrast, leaving the main road with its cafes, petrol pumps, factories and management institutes and entering the rural hinterland where very little had changed in a hundred years. Women worked in the fields, old men smoked hookahs in their courtyards, and a few children were playing *guli-danda* instead of cricket! It brought home to me the reality of India—urban life and rural life are still poles apart.

These journeys are seldom without incident. I was sipping a coffee at a wayside restaurant, when a foreign woman walked in, and asked the waiter if they had '*à la carte*'. Roadside stops seldom provide menus, nor do they go in for French, but our waiter wanted to be helpful, so he led the tourist outside and showed her the way to the public toilet. As she did not return to the restaurant, I have no idea if she eventually found *à la carte*.

My driver on a recent trip assured me that he knew Delhi very well and could get me to any destination. I told him I'd been booked into a big hotel near the airport, and gave him the name. Not to worry, he told me, and drove confidently towards Palam. There he got confused, and after taking several unfamiliar turnings, drove straight into a large piggery situated behind the airport. We were surrounded by some fifty or sixty pigs and an equal number of children from the *mohalla*. One boy even asked me if I wanted to purchase a pig. I do like a bit of bacon now and then, but unlike Lord Emsworth I do not have any ambition to breed prize pigs, so I had to decline.

After some arguments over right of way, we were allowed to proceed and finally made it to the hotel.

Occasionally I have shared a taxi with another passenger, but after one or two disconcerting experiences I have taken to travelling alone or with a friend.

The last time I shared a taxi with someone, I was pleased to find that my fellow passenger, a large gentleman with a fierce moustache, had bought one of my books, which was lying on the seat between us.

I thought I'd be friendly and so, to break the ice, I remarked 'I see you have one of my books with you,' glancing modestly at the paperback on the seat.

'What do you mean, *your* book?' he bridled, giving me a dirty look. 'I just bought this book at the news agency!'

'No, no,' I stammered, 'I don't mean it's mine, I mean it's my book—er, that is, I happened to write it!'

'Oh, so now you're claiming to be the author!' He looked at me as though I was a fraud of the worst kind. 'What is your real profession, may I ask?'

'I'm just a typist,' I said, and made no further attempt to make friends.

Indeed, I am very careful about trumpeting my literary or other achievements, as I am frequently misunderstood.

Recently, at a book reading in New Delhi, a little girl asked me how many books I'd written.

'Oh, about sixty or seventy,' I said quite truthfully.

At which another child piped up: 'Why can't you be a little modest about it?'

Sometimes you just can't win.

My author's ego received a salutary beating when on one of my earlier trips, I stopped at a small book-stall and looked around, hoping (like any other author) to spot one of my books. Finally, I found one, under a pile of books by Deepak Chopra, Khushwant Singh, William Dalrymple and other luminaries. I slipped it out from the bottom of the pile and surreptitiously placed it on top.

Unfortunately the bookseller had seen me do this.

He picked up the offending volume and returned it to the bottom of the pile, saying 'No demand for this book, sir'.

I wasn't going to tell him I was the author. But just to prove him wrong, I bought the poor neglected thing.

'This is a collector's item,' I told him.

'Ah,' he said, 'At last I meet a collector.'

The number of interesting people I meet on the road is matched only by the number of interesting drivers who have carried me back and forth in their chariots of fire.

The last to do so, the driver of a Qualis, must have had ambitions to be an air pilot. He used the road as a runway and was constantly on the verge of taking off. Pedestrians, cyclists, and drivers of smaller vehicles scattered to left and right, often hurling abuse at my charioteer, who seemed immune to the most colourful invectives. Trucks did not give way but he simply swerved around them, adopting a zigzag approach to the task of getting from Delhi to Dehradun in the shortest possible time.

'There's no hurry,' I told him more than once, but his English was limited and he told me later that he thought I was saying 'Please hurry!'

Well, he hurried and he harried until at a railway-crossing where we were forced to stop, an irate scooterist came abreast and threatened to turn the driver over to the police. A long and heated argument followed, and it appeared that there would soon be a punch-up, when the crossing-gate suddenly opened and the Qualis flew forward, leaving the fuming scooterist far behind.

As I do not drive myself, I am normally the ideal person to have in the front seat; I repose complete confidence in the man behind the wheel. And sitting up front, I see more of the road and the passing scene.

One of Mussoorie's better drivers is Sardar Manmohan Singh who drives his own taxi. He is also a keen wildlife enthusiast. It always amazes me how he is able to drive through the Siwaliks, on a winding hill road, and still be able to keep his eye open for denizens of the surrounding forest.

'See that cheetal!' he will exclaim, or 'What a fine sambhar!' or 'Just look at that elephant!'

All this at high speed. And before I've had time to get more than a fleeting glimpse of one of these creatures, we are well past them.

Manmohan swears that he has seen a tiger crossing the road near the Mohand Pass, and as he is a person of some integrity, I have to believe him. I think the tiger appears especially for Manmohan.

Another wildlife enthusiast is my old friend Vishal Ohri, of State Bank fame. On one occasion he drove me down a forest road between Hardwar and Mohand, and we did indeed see a number of animals, cheetal and wild boar.

Unlike our car drivers, he was in no hurry to reach our destination and would stop every now and then, in order to examine the footprints of elephants. He also pointed out large dollops of fresh elephant dung, proof that wild elephants were in the vicinity. I did not think his old Fiat would out-run an angry elephant and urged him to get a move on before nightfall. Vishal then held forth on the benefits of elephant dung and how it could be used to reinforce mud walls. I assured him that I would try it out on the walls of my study, which was in danger of falling down.

Vishal was well ahead of his time. Only the other day I read in one of our papers that elephant dung could be converted into good quality paper. Perhaps they'll use it to make bank notes. Reserve Bank, please note.

★

Other good drivers who have taken me here and there include Ganesh Saili, who is even better after a few drinks; Victor Banerjee who is better before drinks; and young Harpreet who is a fan of Kenny G's saxophone playing. On the road to Delhi with Harpreet, I had six hours of listening to Kenny G on tape. On my return, two days later, I had another six hours of Kenny G. Now I go into a frenzy whenever I hear a saxophone.

My publisher has an experienced old driver who also happens to be quite deaf. He blares the car horn vigorously and without respite. When I asked him why he used the horn so much, he replied, 'Well, I can't hear *their* horns, but I'll make sure they hear mine!' As good a reason as any.

It is sometimes said that women don't make good drivers, but I beg to differ. Mrs Biswas was an excellent driver but a dangerous woman to know. Her husband had been a well-known shikari, and he kept a stuffed panther in the drawing room of his Delhi farm-house. Mrs Biswas spent the occasional weekend at her summer home in Landour. I'd been to one or two of her parties, attended mostly by menfolk.

One day, while I was loitering on the road, she drove up and asked me if I'd like to accompany her down to Dehradun.

'I'll come with you,' I said, 'provided we can have a nice lunch at Kwality.'

So down the hill we glided, and Mrs Biswas did some shopping, and we lunched at Kwality, and got back into her

car and set off again—but in a direction opposite to Mussoorie and Landour.

'Where are we going?' I asked.

'To Delhi, of course. Aren't you coming with me?'

'I didn't know we were going to Delhi. I don't even have my pyjamas with me.'

'Don't worry,' said Mrs B. 'My husband's pyjamas will fit you.'

'He may not want me to wear his pyjamas,' I protested.

'Oh, don't worry. He's in London just now.'

I persuaded Mrs Biswas to stop at the nearest bus stop, bid her farewell, and took the bus back to Mussoorie. She may have been a good driver but I had no intention of ending up stuffed alongside the stuffed panther in the drawing room.

THREE

Cold Beer at Chutmalpur

Just outside the small market town of Chutmalpur (on the way back from Delhi) one is greeted by a large signboard with just two words on it: Cold Beer. The signboard is almost as large as the shop from which the cold beer is dispensed; but after a gruelling five-hour drive from Delhi, in the heat and dust of May, a glass of chilled beer is welcome—except, of course, to teetotallers who will find other fizzy ways to satiate their thirst.

Chutmalpur is not the sort of place you'd choose to retire in. But it has its charms, not the least of which is its Sunday Market, when the varied produce of the rural interior finds its way on to the dusty pavements, and the air vibrates with noise, colour and odours. Carpets of red chillies, seasonal fruits, stacks of grain and vegetables, cheap toys for the children, bangles of lac, wooden artifacts, colourful underwear, sweets of every description, *churan* to go with them...

'*Lakar hajam, pather hajam!*' cries the churan-seller. Translated: Digest wood, digest stones! That is, if you partake of this particular digestive pill which, when I tried it, appeared to be one part *hing* (asafoetida) and one part gunpowder.

Things are seldom what they seem to be. Passing through the small town of Purkazi, I noticed a sign-board which announced the availability of 'Books'—just that. Intrigued, I stopped to find out more about this bookshop in the wilderness. Perhaps I'd find a rare tome to add to my library. Peeping in, I discovered that the dark interior was stacked from floor to ceiling with exercise books! Apparently the shop-owner was the supplier for the district.

Rare books can be seen in Roorkee, in the University's old library. Here, not many years ago, a First Folio Shakespeare turned up and was celebrated in the Indian Press as a priceless discovery. Perhaps it's still there.

Also in the library is a bust of Sir Proby Cautley, who conceived and built the Ganga Canal, which starts at Hardwar and passes through Roorkee on its way across the Doab. Hardly anyone today has heard of Cautley, and yet surely his achievement outstrips that of many Englishmen in India—soldiers and statesmen who became famous for doing all the wrong things.

Cautley's Canal

Cautley came to India at the age of seventeen and joined the Bengal Artillery. In 1825, he assisted Captain Robert Smith, the engineer in charge of constructing the Eastern Yamuna Canal. By 1836 he was Superintendent-General of Canals. From the start, he worked towards his dream of building a Ganga Canal, and spent six months walking and riding through the jungles and countryside, taking each level and measurement himself, sitting up all night to transfer them to his maps. He was confident that a 500-kilometre canal was feasible. There were many objections and obstacles to his project, most of them financial, but Cautley persevered and eventually persuaded the East India Company to back him.

Digging of the canal began in 1839. Cautley had to make his own bricks—millions of them—his own brick kiln, and his own mortar. A hundred thousand tonnes of lime went into the mortar, the other main ingredient of which was *surkhi*, made by grinding over-burnt bricks to a powder. To reinforce the mortar, *ghur*, ground lentils and jute fibres were added to it.

Initially, opposition came from the priests in Hardwar, who felt that the waters of the holy Ganga would be imprisoned. Cautley pacified them by agreeing to leave a narrow gap in the dam through which the river water could flow unchecked. He won over the priests when he inaugurated his project with *aarti*, and the worship of Ganesh, God of Good Beginnings. He also undertook the repair of the sacred bathing ghats along the river. The canal banks were also to have their own ghats with steps leading down to the water.

The headworks of the Canal are at Hardwar, where the Ganga enters the plains after completing its majestic journey through the Himalayas. Below Hardwar, Cautley had to dig new courses for some of the mountain torrents that threatened the canal. He collected them into four steams and took them over the Canal by means of four passages. Near Roorkee, the land fell away sharply and here Cautley had to build an aqueduct, a masonry bridge that carries the Canal for half a kilometre across the Solani torrent—a unique engineering feat. At Roorkee the Canal is twenty-five metres higher than the parent river which flows almost parallel to it.

Most of the excavation work on the canal was done mainly by the Oads, a gypsy tribe who were professional diggers for most of northwest India. They took great pride in their work. Through extremely poor, Cautley found them a happy and carefree lot who worked in a very organized manner.

When the Canal was formally opened on the 8th April 1854, its main channel was 348 miles long, its branches 306 and the distributaries over 3,000. Over 767,000 acres in 5,000 villages were irrigated. One of its main branches re-entered the Ganga at Kanpur; it also had branches to Fatehgarh, Bulandshahr and Aligarh.

Cautley's achievements did not end there. He was also actively involved in Dr Falconer's fossil expedition in the Siwaliks. He presented to the British Museum an extensive collection of fossil mammalia—including hippopotamus and crocodile fossils, evidence that the region was once swampland or an inland sea. Other animal remains found here included the sabre-toothed tiger; *Elephis ganesa*, an elephant with a trunk ten-and-a-half feet long; a three-toed ancestor of the horse; the bones of a fossil ostrich; and the remains of giant cranes and tortoises. Exciting times, exciting finds.

Nor did Cautley's interests and activities end in fossil excavation. My copy of Surgeon General Balfour's Cyclopedia of India (1873) lists a number of fascinating reports and papers by Cautley. He wrote on a submerged city, twenty feet underground, near Behut in the Doab; on the coal and lignite in the Himalayas; on gold washings in the Siwalik Hills, between the Jamuna and Sutlej rivers; on a new species of snake; on the mastodons of the Siwaliks; on the manufacture of tar; and on *Panchukkis* or corn mills.

How did he find time for all this, I wonder. Most of his life was spent in tents, overseeing the canal work or digging up fossils. He had a house in Mussoorie (one of the first), but he could not have spent much time in it. It is today part of the Manav Bharti School, and there is still a plaque in the office stating that Cautley lived there. Perhaps he wrote some of his reports and expositions during brief sojourns in the hills. It is said that his wife left him, unable to compete against the rival attractions of canals and fossils remains.

I wonder, too, if there was any follow up on his reports of the submerged city—is it still there, waiting to be rediscovered—or his findings on gold washings in the Siwaliks. Should my royalties ever dry up, I might just wonder off into the Siwaliks, looking for 'gold in them thar hills'. Meanwhile, whenever I travel by road from Delhi to Hardwar, and pass over that placid Canal at various places en-route, I think of the man who spent more than twenty years of his life in executing this magnificent project, and others equally demanding. And then, his work done, walking away from it all without thought of fame or fortune.

A Jungle Princess

From Roorkee separate roads lead to Hardwar, Saharanpur, Dehradun. And from the Saharanpur road you can branch off to Paonta Sahib, with its famous gurudwara glistening above the blue waters of the Yamuna. Still blue up here, but not so blue by the time it enters Delhi. Industrial affluents and human waste soon muddy the purest of rivers.

From Paonta you can turn right to Herbertpur, a small township originally settled by an Anglo-Indian family early in the nineteenth century. As may be inferred by its name, Herbert was the scion of the family, but I have been unable to discover much about him. When I was a boy, the Carberry family owned much of the land around here, but by the time Independence came, only one of the family remained—Doreen, a sultry,

dusky beauty who become known in Dehra as the 'Jungle Princess'. Her husband had deserted her, but she had a small daughter who grew up on the land. Doreen's income came from her mango and guava orchards, and she seemed quite happy living in this isolated rural area near the river. Occasionally she came into Dehra Dun, a bus ride of a couple of hours, and she would visit my mother, a childhood friend, and occasionally stay overnight.

On one occasion we went to Doreen's jungle home for a couple of days. I was just seven or eight years old. I remember Doreen's daughter (about my age) teaching me to climb trees. I managed the guava tree quite well, but some of the others were too difficult for me.

How did this jungle queen manage to live by herself in this remote area, where her house, orchard and fields were bordered by forest on one side and the river on the other?

Well, she had her servants of course, and they were loyal to her. And she also possessed several guns, and could handle them very well. I saw her bring down a couple of pheasants with her twelve-bore spread shot. She had also killed a cattle-lifting tiger which had been troubling a nearby village, and a marauding leopard that had taken one of her dogs. So she was quite capable of taking care of herself. When I last saw her, some twenty-five years ago, she was in her seventies. I believe she sold her land and went to live elsewhere with her daughter, who by then had a family of her own.

FOUR

The Kipling Road

Remember the old road,
The steep stony path
That took us up from Rajpur,
Toiling and sweating
And grumbling at the climb,
But enjoying it all the same.
At first the hills were hot and bare,
But then there were trees near Jharipani
And we stopped at the Halfway House
And swallowed lungfuls of diamond-cut air.
Then onwards, upwards, to the town,
Our appetites to repair!

Well, no one uses the old road any more.
Walking is out of fashion now.
And if you have a car to take you
Swiftly up the motor-road

Why bother to toil up a disused path?
You'd have to be an old romantic like me
To want to take that route again.
But I did it last year,
Pausing and plodding and gasping for air—
Both road and I being a little worse for wear!
But I made it to the top and stopped to rest
And looked down to the valley and the silver stream
Winding its way towards the plains.
And the land stretched out before me, and the years fell
away,
And I was a boy again,
And the friends of my youth were there beside me,
And nothing had changed.

'Remember the Old Road'

As boys we would often trudge up from Rajpur to Mussoorie by the old bridle-path, the road that used to serve the hill-station in the days before the motor road was built. Before 1900, the traveller to Mussoorie took a tonga from Saharanpur to Dehradun, spent the night at a Rajpur hotel, and the following day came up the steep seven-mile path on horseback, or on foot, or in a dandy (a crude palanquin) held aloft by two, sometimes four, sweating coolies.

The railway came to Dehradun in 1904, and a few years later the first motor car made it to Mussoorie, the motor road following the winding contours and hairpin bends of the old bullock-cart road. Rajpur went out of business; no one stopped there any more, the hotels became redundant, and the bridle-path was seldom used except by those of us who thought it would be fun to come up on foot.

For the first two or three miles you walked in the hot sun, along a treeless path. It was only at Jharipani (at approximately 4,000 ft.) that the oak forests began, providing shade and shelter. Situated on a spur of its own, was the Railways school, Oakgrove, still there today, providing a boarding-school education to the children of Railway personnel. My mother and her sisters came from a Railway family, and all of them studied at Oakgrove in the 1920's. So did a male cousin, who succumbed to cerebral malaria during the school term. In spite of the salubrious climate, mortality was high amongst school children. There were no cures then for typhoid, cholera, malaria, dysentery and other infectious diseases.

Above Oakgrove was Fairlawn, the palace of the Nepali royal family. There was a sentry box outside the main gate, but there was never any sentry in it, and on more than one occasion I took shelter there from the rain. Today it's a series of cottages, one of which belongs to *Outlook*'s editor, Vinod Mehta, who seeks shelter there from the heat and dust of Delhi.

From Jharapani we climbed to Barlowganj, where another venerable institution St George's College, crowns the hilltop. Then on to Bala Hissar, once the home-in-exile of an Afghan king, and now the grounds of Wynberg-Allen, another school. In later years I was to live near this school, and it was its then Principal, Rev W. Biggs, who told me that the bridle-path was once known as the Kipling Road.

Why was that, I asked. Had Kipling ever come up that way? Rev Biggs wasn't sure, but he referred me to *Kim*, and the chapter in which Kim and the Lama leave the plains for the hills. It begins thus:

They had crossed the Siwaliks and the half-tropical Doon, left Mussoorie behind them, and headed north along the narrow hill-roads. Day after day they struck deeper into the huddled mountains, and day after day Kim watched the lama return to a man's strength. Among the terraces of the Doon he had leaned on the boy's shoulder, ready to profit by wayside halts. Under the great ramp to Mussoorie he drew himself together as an old hunter faces a well remembered bank, and where he should have sunk exhausted swung his long draperies about him, drew a deep double-lungful of the diamond air, and walked as only a hillman can.

This description is accurate enough, but it is not evidence that Kipling actually came this way, and his geography becomes quite confusing in the subsequent pages—as Peter Hopkirk discovered when he visited Mussoorie a few years ago, retracing Kim's journeys for his book *Quest for Kim*. Hopkirk spent some

time with me in this little room where I am now writing, but
we were unable to establish the exact route that Kim and the
Lama took after traversing Mussoorie. Presumably they had
come up the bridle-path. But then? After that, Kipling becomes
rather vague.

Mussoorie does not really figure in Rudyard Kipling's prose
or poetry. The Simla Hills were his beat. As a journalist he was
a regular visitor to Simla, then the summer seat of the British
Raj.

But last year my Swiss friend, Anilees Goel, brought me
proof that Kipling had indeed visited Mussoorie. Among his
unpublished papers and other effects in the Library of Congress,
there exists an album of photographs, which includes two of
the Charleville Hotel, Mussoorie, where he had spent the
summer of 1888. On a photograph of the office he had inscribed
these words:

> And there were men with a thousand wants
> And women with babes galore
> But the dear little angels in Heaven know
> That Wutzler *never* swore.

Wutzler was the patient, long-suffering manager of this
famous hotel, now the premises of the Lal Bahadur Shastri
National Academy of Administration.

A second photograph is inscribed with the caption 'Quarters
at the Charleville, April-July 88,' and carries this verse:

A burning sun in cloudless skies
and April dies,
A dusty Mall—three sunsets splendid
and May is ended,
Grey mud beneath—grey cloud o'erhead
and June is dead.
A little bill in late July
And then we fly.

Pleasant enough, but hardly great verse, and I'm not surprised that Kipling did not publish these lines.

However, we now know that he came to Mussoorie and spent some time here, and that he would have come up by the old bridle-path (there was no other way except by bullock-cart on the long and tortuous cast road), and Rev Biggs and others were right in calling it the Kipling Road, although officially that was never its name.

As you climb up from Barlowganj, you pass a number of pretty cottages—May Cottage, Wakefield, Ralston Manor, Wayside Hall—and these old houses all have stories to tell, for they have stood mute witness to the comings and goings of all manner of people.

Take Ralston Manor. It was witness to an impromptu cremation, probably Mussoorie's first European cremation, in the late 1890's. There is a small chapel in the grounds of Ralston, and the story goes that a Mr and Mrs Smallman had been living in the house, and Mr Smallman had expressed a wish to be cremated at his death. When he died, his widow decided to observe his wishes and had her servants build a funeral pyre in the garden. The cremation was well underway when someone rode by and looked in to see what was happening. The unauthorised cremation was reported to the authorities and Mrs Smallman had to answer some awkward questions. However, she was let off with a warning (a warning not to cremate any future husbands?) and later she built the little chapel on the site of the funeral pyre—in gratitude or as penance, or as a memorial, we are not told. But the chapel is still there, and this little tale is recorded in *Chowkidar* (Autumn 1995), the journal of the British Association for Cemeteries in South Asia (BACSA).

As we move further up the road, keeping to the right, we come to Wayside Hall and Wayside Cottage, which have the advantage of an open sunny hillside and views to the north and east. I lived in the cottage for a couple of years, back in 1966-67, as a tenant of the Powell sisters who lived in the Hall.

There were three sisters, all in their seventies; they had survived their husbands. Annie, the eldest, had a son who lived abroad, Martha, the second, did not have children; Dr Simmonds, the third sister, had various adopted children who came to see her from time to time. They were God-fearing, religious folk, but not bigots; never chided me for not going to church. Annie's teas were marvellous; snacks and savouries in abundance.

They kept a beautiful garden.

'Why go to church?' I said. 'Your garden is a church.'

In spring and summer it was awash with poppies, petunia, phlox, larkspur, calendula, snapdragons and other English flowers. During the monsoon, the gladioli took over, while magnificent dahlias reared up from the rich foliage. During the autumn came zinnias and marigolds and cosmos. And even during the winter months there would be geraniums and primulae blooming in the verandah.

Honeysuckle climbed the wall outside my window, filling my bedroom with its heady scent. And wisteria grew over the main gate. There was perfume in the air.

Annie herself smelt of freshly baked bread. Dr Simmonds smelt of Pears' baby soap. Martha smelt of apples. All good smells, emanating from good people.

Although they lived on their own, without any men on the premises, they never felt threatened or insecure. Mussoorie was a safe place to live in then, and still is to a great extent—much safer than towns in the plains, where the crime rate keeps pace with the population growth.

Annie's son, Gerald, then in his sixties, did come out to see them occasionally. He had been something of a shikari in his youth—or so he claimed—and told me he could call up a panther from the valley without any difficulty. To do this, he made a contraption out of an old packing-case, with a hole bored in the middle, then he passed a length of thick wire through the hole, and by moving the wire backwards and forward produced a sound not dissimilar to the sawing, coughing sound made by a panther during the mating season. (Incidentally, a panther and a leopard are the same animal.)

Gerry invited me to join him on a steep promontory overlooking a little stream. I did so with some trepidation. Hunting had never been my forte, and normally I preferred to go along with Ogden Nash's dictum, 'If you meet a panther, don't anther!'

However, Gerry's gun looked powerful enough, and I believed him when he told me he was a crack shot. I have always taken people at their word. One of my failings I suppose.

Anyway, we positioned ourselves on this ledge, and Gerry started producing panther noises with his box. His Master's Voice would have been proud of it. Nothing happened for about twenty minutes, and I was beginning to lose patience when we were answered by the cough and grunt of what could only have been a panther. But we couldn't see it! Gerry produced a pair of binoculars and trained them on some distant object below, which turned out to be a goat. The growling continued—and then it was just above us! The panther had made a detour and was now standing on a rock and staring down, no doubt wondering which of us was making such attractive mating calls.

Gerry swung round, raised his gun and fired. He missed by a couple of feet, and the panther bounded away, no doubt disgusted with the proceedings.

We returned to Wayside Hall, and revived ourselves with brandy and soda.

'We'll get it next time, old chap,' said Gerry. But although we tried, the panther did not put in another appearance. Gerry's panther call sounded genuine enough, but neither he nor I nor his wired box looked anything like a female panther.

FIVE

At the End of the Road

Choose your companions carefully when you are walking in the hills. If you are accompanied by the wrong person—by which I mean someone who is temperamentally very different to you—that long hike you've been dreaming of could well turn into a nightmare.

This has happened to me more than once. The first time, many years ago, when I accompanied a businessman-friend to the Pindari Glacier in Kumaon. He was in such a hurry to get back to his executive's desk in Delhi that he set off for the Glacier as though he had a train to catch, refusing to spend any time admiring the views, looking for birds or animals, or greeting the local inhabitants. By the time we had left the last dak bungalow at Phurkia, I was ready to push him over a cliff. He probably felt the same way about me.

On our way down, we met a party of Delhi University boys who were on the same trek. They were doing it in a leisurely, good-humoured fashion. They were very friendly and asked me to join them. On an impulse, I bid farewell to my previous companion—who was only too glad to dash off downhill to where his car was parked at Kapkote—while I made a second ascent to the Glacier, this time in better company.

Unfortunately, my previous companion had been the one with the funds. My new friends fed me on the way back, and in Naini Tal I pawned my watch so that I could have enough for the bus ride back to Delhi. Lesson Two: always carry enough money with you; don't depend on a wealthy friend!

Of course, it's hard to know who will be a 'good companion' until you have actually hit the road together. Sharing a meal or having a couple of drinks together is not the same as tramping along on a dusty road with the water bottle down to its last drop. You can't tell until you have spent a night in the rain, or lost the way in the mountains, or finished all the food, whether both of you have stout hearts and a readiness for the unknown.

I like walking alone, but a good companion is well worth finding. He will add to the experience. 'Give me a companion of my way, be it only to mention how the shadows lengthen as the sun declines,' wrote Hazlitt.

Pratap was one such companion. He had invited me to spend a fortnight with him in his village above the Nayar river in Pauri-Garhwal. In those days, there was no motor-road beyond Lansdowne and one had to walk some thirty miles to get to the village.

But first, one had to get to Lansdowne. This involved getting into a train at Dehra Dun, getting out at Luxor (across the Ganga), getting into another train, and then getting out again at Najibabad and waiting for a bus to take one through the Tarai to Kotdwara.

Najibabad must have been one of the least inspiring places on earth. Hot, dusty, apparently lifeless. We spent two hours at the bus-stand, in the company of several donkeys, also quartered there. We were told that the area had once been the favourite hunting ground of a notorious dacoit, Sultana Daku, whose fortress overlooked the barren plain. I could understand him taking up dacoity—what else was there to do in such a place—and presumed that he looked elsewhere for his loot, for in Nazibabad there was nothing worth taking. In due course he was betrayed and hanged by the British, when they should instead have given him an OBE for stirring up the sleepy countryside.

There was a short branch line from Nazibabad to Kotdwara, but the train wasn't leaving that day, as the engine driver was unaccountably missing. The bus-driver seemed to be missing too, but he did eventually turn up, a little worse for some late night drinking. I could sympathize with him. If in 1940, Nazibabad drove you to dacoity, in 1960 it drove you to drink.

Kotdwara, a steamy little town in the foothills, was equally depressing. It seemed to lack any sort of character. Here we changed buses, and moved into higher regions, and the higher we went, the nicer the surroundings; by the time we reached Lansdowne, at six thousand feet, we were in good spirits.

The small hill-station was a recruiting centre for the Garhwal Rifles (and still is), and did not cater to tourists. There were no hotels, just a couple of tea-stalls where a meal of dal and rice could be obtained. I believe it is much the same forty years on. Pratap had a friend who was the caretaker of an old, little used church, and he bedded us down in the vestry. Early next morning we set out on our long walk to Pratap's village.

I have covered longer distances on foot, but not all in one day. Thirty miles of trudging up hill and down and up again, most of it along a footpath that traversed bare hillsides where the hot May sun beat down relentlessly. Here and there we found a little shade and a freshet of spring water, which kept us going; but we had neglected to bring food with us apart from a couple of rock-hard buns probably dating back to colonial times, which we had picked up in Lansdowne. We were lucky to meet a farmer who gave us some onions and accompanied us part of the way.

Onions for lunch? Nothing better when you're famished.

In the West they say, 'Never talk to strangers.' In the East they say, 'Always talk to strangers.' It was this stranger who gave us sustenance on the road, just as strangers had given me company on the way to the Pindar Glacier. On the open road there are no strangers. You share the same sky, the same mountain, the same sunshine and shade. On the open road we are all brothers.

The stranger went his way, and we went ours. 'Just a few more bends,' according to Pratap, always encouraging to the novice plainsman. But I was to be a hillman by the time we returned to Dehra! Hundreds of 'just a few more bends,' before we reached the village, and I kept myself going with my off-key rendering of the old Harry Lauder song—

'Keep right on to the end of the road,
Keep right on to the end.
If your way be long, let your heart be strong,
So keep right on round the bend.'

By the time we'd done the last bend, I had a good idea of how the expression 'going round the bend' had came into existence. A maddened climber, such as I, had to negotiate one bend too many....

But Pratap was the right sort of companion. He adjusted his pace to suit mine; never lost patience; kept telling me I was a great walker. We arrived at the village just as night fell, and there was his mother waiting for us with a tumbler of milk.

Milk! I'd always hated the stuff (and still do) but that day I was grateful for it and drank two glasses. Fortunately it was cold. There was plenty of milk for me to drink during my two-week stay in the village, as Pratap's family possessed at least three productive cows. The milk was supplemented by thick rotis, made from grounded maize, seasonal vegetables, rice, and a species of lentil peculiar to the area and very difficult to digest. Health food friends would have approved of this fare, but it did not agree with me, and I found myself constipated most of the time. Still, better to be constipated than to be in free flow.

The point I am making is that it is always wise to carry your own food on a long hike or treks in the hills. Not that I could have done so, as Pratap's guest; he would have taken it as an insult. By the time I got back to Dehra—after another exhausted trek, and more complicated bus and train journeys— I felt quite famished and out of sorts. I bought some eggs and bacon rashers from the grocery store across the road from Astley Hall, and made myself a scrumptious breakfast. I am not much of a cook, but I can fry an egg and get the bacon nice and crisp. My needs are simple really. To each his own!

On another trek, from Mussoorie to Chamba (before the motor-road came into existence) I put two tins of sardines into my knapsack but forgot to take along a can-opener. Three days later I was back in Dehra, looking very thin indeed, and with my sardine tins still intact. That night I ate the contents of both tins.

Reading an account of the same trek undertaken by John Lang about a hundred years earlier, I was awestruck by his description of the supplies that he and his friends took with them.

Here he is, writing in Charles Dickens' magazine, *Household Words*, in the issue of January 30, 1858:

> In front of the club-house our marching establishment had collected, and the one hundred and fifty coolies were laden with the baggage and stores. There were tents...camp tables, chairs, beds, bedding, boxes of every kind, dozens of cases of wine—port, sherry and claret—beer, ducks, fowls, geese, guns, umbrellas, great coats and the like.

He then goes on to talk of lobsters, oysters and preserved soups.

I doubt if I would have got very far on such fare. I took the same road in October, 1958, a century later; on my own and without provisions except for the afore-mentioned sardine tins. By dusk I had reached the village of Kaddukhal, where the local shopkeeper put me up for the might.

I slept on the floor, on a sheepskin infested by fleas. They were all over me as soon as I lay down, and I found it impossible to sleep. I fled the shop before dawn.

'Don't go out before daylight,' warned my host. 'There are bears around.'

But I would sooner have faced a bear than that onslaught from the denizens of the sheepskin. And I reached Chamba in time for an early morning cup of tea.

★

Most Himalayan villages lie in the valleys, where there are small streams, some farmland, and protection from the biting winds that come through the mountain passes. The houses are usually made of large stones, and have sloping slate roofs so the heavy monsoon rain can run off easily. During the sunny autumn months, the roofs are often covered with pumpkins, left there to ripen in the sun.

One October night, when I was sleeping at a friend's house just off the Tehri road, I was awakened by a rumbling and thumping on the roof. I woke my friend Jai and asked him what was happening.

'It's only a bear,' he said.

'Is it trying to get in?'

'No. It's after the pumpkins.'

A little later, when we looked out of a window, we saw a black bear making off through a field, leaving a trail of half-eaten pumpkins.

In winter, when snow covers the higher ranges, the Himalayan bears descend to lower altitudes in search of food. Sometimes they forage in fields. And because they are shortsighted and suspicious of anything that moves, they can be dangerous. But, like most wild animals, they avoid humans as much as possible.

Village folk always advise me to run downhill if chased by a bear. They say bears find it easier to run uphill than down. I have yet to be chased by a bear, and will happily skip the experience. But I have seen a few of these mountain bears and they are always fascinating to watch.

Himalayan bears enjoy corn, pumpkins, plums, and apricots. Once, while I was sitting in an oak tree on Pari Tibba, hoping to see a pair of pine-martens that lived nearby, I heard the whining grumble of a bear, and presently a small bear ambled into the clearing beneath the tree.

He was little more than a cub, and I was not alarmed. I sat very still, waiting to see what the bear would do.

He put his nose to the ground and sniffed his way along until he came to a large anthill. Here he began huffing and puffing, blowing rapidly in and out of his nostrils so that the dust from the anthill flew in all directions. But the anthill had been deserted, and so, grumbling, the bear made his way up a nearby plum tree. Soon he was perched high in the branches. It was then that he saw me.

The bear at once scrambled several feet higher up the tree and lay flat on a branch. Since it wasn't a very big branch, there was a lot of bear showing on either side. He tucked his head behind another branch. He could no longer see me, so he apparently was satisfied that he was hidden, although he couldn't help grumbling.

Like all bears, this one was full of curiosity. So, slowly, inch by inch, his black snout appeared over the edge of the branch. As soon as he saw me, he drew his head back and hid his face.

He did this several times. I waited until he wasn't looking, then moved some way down my tree. When the bear looked over and saw that I was missing, he was so pleased that he stretched right across to another branch and helped himself to a plum. At that, I couldn't help bursting into laughter.

The startled young bear tumbled out of the tree, dropped through the branches some fifteen feet, and landed with a thump in a pile of dried leaves. He was unhurt, but fled from the clearing, grunting and squealing all the way.

Another time, my friend Jai told me that a bear had been active in his cornfield. We took up a post at night in an old cattle shed, which gave a clear view of the moonlit field.

A little after midnight, the bear came down to the edge of the field. She seemed to sense that we had been about. She was hungry, however. So, after standing on her hind legs and peering around to make sure the field was empty, she came cautiously out of the forest.

The bear's attention was soon distracted by some Tibetan prayer flags, which had been strung between two trees. She gave a grunt of disapproval and began to back away, but the fluttering of the flags was a puzzle that she wanted to solve. So she stopped and watched them.

Soon the bear advanced to within a few feet of the flags, examining them from various angles. Then, seeing that they posed no danger, she went right up to the flags and pulled them down. Grunting with apparent satisfaction, she moved into the field of corn.

Jai had decided that he didn't want to lose any more of his crop, so he started shouting. His children woke up and soon came running from the house, banging on empty kerosene tins.

Deprived of her dinner, the bear made off in a bad temper. She ran downhill at a good speed, and I was glad that I was not in her way.

Uphill or downhill, an angry bear is best given a very wide path.

Sleeping out, under the stars, is a very romantic conception. 'Stones thy pillow, earth thy bed,' goes an old hymn, but a rolled up towel or shirt will make a more comfortable pillow. Do not settle down to sleep on sloping ground, as I did once when I was a Boy Scout during my prep-school days. We had camped at Tara Devi, on the outskirts of Shimla, and as it was a warm night I decided to sleep outside our tent. In the middle of the night I began to roll. Once you start rolling on a steep hillside, you don't stop. Had it not been for a thorny dog-rose bush, which halted my descent, I might well have rolled over the edge of a precipice.

I had a wonderful night once, sleeping on the sand on the banks of the Ganga above Rishikesh. It was a balmy night, with just a faint breeze blowing across the river, and as I lay

there looking up at the stars, the lines of a poem by R.L.
Stevenson kept running through my head:

> Give to me the life I love,
> Let the lave go by me,
> Give the jolly heaven above
> And the byway nigh me.
> Bed in the bush with stars to see,
> Bread I dip in the river—
> There's the life for a man like me,
> There's the life for ever.

The following night I tried to repeat the experience, but
the jolly heaven above opened up in the early hours, the rain
came pelting down, and I had to run for shelter to the nearest
Ashram. Never take Mother Nature for granted!

The best kind of walk, and this applies to the plains as well
as to the hills, is the one in which you have no particular
destination when you set out.

'Where are you off?' asked a friend of me the other day,
when he met me on the road.

'Honestly, I have no idea,' I said, and I was telling the truth.

I did end up in Happy Valley, where I met an old friend
whom I hadn't seen for years. When we were boys, his mother
used to tell us stories about the bhoots that haunted her village
near Mathura. We reminisced and then went our different
ways. I took the road to Hathipaon and met a schoolgirl who

covered ten miles every day on her way to and from her school. So there were still people who used their legs, though out of necessity rather than choice.

Anyway, she gave me a story to write and thus I ended the day with two stories, one a memoir and the other based on a fresh encounter. And all because I had set out without a plan. The adventure is not in getting somewhere, it's the on-the-way experience. It is not the expected; it's the surprise. Not the fulfilment of prophecy, but the providence of something better than that prophesied.

SIX

Sacred Shrines Along the Way

Nandprayag: Where Rivers Meet

It's a funny thing, but long before I arrive at a place I can usually tell whether I am going to like it or not.

Thus, while I was still some twenty miles from the town of Pauri, I felt it was not going to be my sort of place; and sure enough, it wasn't. On the other hand, while Nandprayag was still out of sight, I knew I was going to like it. And I did.

Perhaps it's something on the wind—emanations of an atmosphere—that are carried to me well before I arrive at my destination. I can't really explain it, and no doubt it is silly to make judgements in advance. But it happens and I mention the fact for what it's worth.

As for Nandprayag, perhaps I'd been there in some previous existence, I felt I was nearing home as soon as we drove into this cheerful roadside hamlet, some little way above the

Nandakini's confluence with the Alakananda river. A *prayag* is a meeting place of two rivers, and as there are many rivers in the Garhwal Himalayas, all linking up to join either the Ganga or the Jamuna, it follows that there are numerous *prayags*, in themselves places of pilgrimage as well as wayside halts enroute to the higher Hindu shrines at Kedarnath and Badrinath. Nowhere else in the Himalayas are there so many temples, sacred streams, holy places and holy men.

Some little way above Nandprayag's busy little bazaar, is the tourist rest-house, perhaps the nicest of the tourist lodges in this region. It has a well-kept garden surrounded by fruit trees and is a little distance from the general hubbub of the main road.

Above it is the old pilgrim path, on which you walked. Just a few decades ago, if you were a pilgrim intent on finding salvation at the abode of the gods, you travelled on foot all the way from the plains, covering about 200 miles in a couple of months. In those days people had the time, the faith and the endurance. Illness and misadventure often dogged their footsteps, but what was a little suffering if at the end of the day they arrived at the very portals of heaven? Some did not survive to make the return journey. Today's pilgrims may not be lacking in devotion, but most of them do expect to come home again.

Along the pilgrim path are several handsome old houses, set among mango trees and the fronds of the papaya and banana. Higher up the hill the pine forests commence, but down here it is almost subtropical. Nandprayag is only about 3,000 feet above sea level—a height at which the vegetation is usually quite lush provided there is protection from the wind.

In one of these double-storeyed houses lives Mr Devki Nandan, scholar and recluse. He welcomes me into his house and plies me with food till I am close to bursting. He has a great love for his little corner of Garhwal and proudly shows me his collection of clippings concerning this area. One of them is from a travelogue by Sister Nivedita—an Englishwoman, Margaret Noble, who became an interpreter of Hinduism to the West. Visiting Nandprayag in 1928, she wrote:

Nandprayag is a place that ought to be famous for its beauty and order. For a mile or two before reaching it we had noticed the superior character of the agriculture and even some careful gardening of fruits and vegetables. The peasantry also, suddenly grew handsome, not unlike the Kashmiris. The town itself is new, rebuilt since the Gohna flood, and its temple stands far out across the fields on the shore of the Prayag. But in this short time a wonderful energy has been at work on architectural carvings, and the little place is full of gemlike beauties. Its temple is dedicated to Naga Takshaka. As the road crosses the river, I noticed two or three old Pathan tombs, the only traces of Mohammedanism that we had seen north of Srinagar in Garhwal.

Little has changed since Sister Nivedita's visit, and there is still a small and thriving Pathan population in Nandprayag. In fact, when I called on Mr Devki Nandan, he was in the act of sending out Id greetings to his Muslim friends. Some of the old graves have disappeared in the debris from new road cuttings: an endless business, this road-building. And as for the beautiful temple described by Sister Nivedita, I was sad to learn that it had been swept away by a mighty flood in 1970, when a cloudburst and subsequent landslide on the Alakananda resulted in great destruction downstream.

Mr Nandan remembers the time when he walked to the small hill-station of Pauri to join the old Messmore Mission School, where so many famous sons of Garhwal received their early education. It would take him four days to get to Pauri. Now it is just four hours by bus. It was only after the Chinese invasion of 1962 that there was a rush of road-building in the hill districts of northern India. Before that, everyone walked and thought nothing of it!

Sitting alone that same evening in the little garden of the rest-house, I heard innumerable birds break into song. I did not see any of them, because the light was fading and the trees were dark, but there was the rather melancholy call of the hill dove, the insistent ascending trill of the koel, and much shrieking, whistling and twittering that I was unable to assign to any particular species.

Now, once again, while I sit on the lawn surrounded by zinnias in full bloom, I am teased by that feeling of having been here before, on this lush hillside, among the pomegranates and oleanders. Is it some childhood memory asserting itself? But as a child I never travelled in these parts.

True, Nandprayag has some affinity with parts of the Doon valley before it was submerged by a tidal wave of humanity. But in the Doon there is no great river running past your garden. Here there are two, and they are also part of this feeling of belonging. Perhaps in some former life I did come this way, or maybe I dreamed about living here. Who knows? Anyway, mysteries are more interesting than certainties. Presently the room-boy joins me for a chat on the lawn. He is in fact running the rest-house in the absence of the manager. A coach-load of pilgrims is due at any moment but until they arrive the place is empty and only the birds can be heard. His name is Janakpal and he tells me something about his village on the next mountain, where a leopard has been carrying off goats and cattle. He doesn't think much of the conservationists' law protecting leopards: nothing can be done unless the animal becomes a man-eater!

A shower of rain descends on us, and so do the pilgrims. Janakpal leaves me to attend to his duties. But I am not left alone for long. A youngster with a cup of tea appears. He wants me to take him to Mussoorie or Delhi. He is fed up, he says, with washing dishes here.

'You are better off here,' I tell him sincerely. 'In Mussoorie you will have twice as many dishes to wash. In Delhi, ten times as many.'

'Yes, but there are cinemas there,' he says, 'and television, and videos.' I am left without an argument. Birdsong may have charms for me but not for the restless dish-washer in Nandprayag. The rain stops and I go for a walk. The pilgrims keep to themselves but the locals are always ready to talk. I remember a saying (and it may have originated in these hills), which goes: 'All men are my friends. I have only to meet them.' In these hills, where life still moves at a leisurely and civilized pace, one is constantly meeting them.

The Magic of Tungnath

The mountains and valleys of Uttaranchal never fail to spring surprises on the traveller in search of the picturesque. It is impossible to know every corner of the Himalaya, which means that there are always new corners to discover; forest or meadow, mountain stream or wayside shrine.

The temple of Tungnath, at a little over 12,000 feet, is the highest shrine on the inner Himalayan range. It lies just below the Chandrashila peak. Some way off the main pilgrim routes, it is less frequented than Kedarnath or Badrinath, although it forms a part of the Kedar temple establishment. The priest here is a local man, a Brahmin from the village of Maku; the other Kedar temples have South Indian priests, a tradition begun by Sankaracharya, the eighth century Hindu reformer and revivalist.

Tungnath's lonely eminence gives it a magic of its own. To get there (or beyond), one passes through some of the most delightful temperate forest in the Garhwal Himalaya. Pilgrim, or trekker, or just plain rambler such as myself, one comes away a better person, forest-refreshed, and more aware of what the world was really like before mankind began to strip it bare.

Duiri Tal, a small lake, lies cradled on the hill above Okhimath, at a height of 8,000 feet. It was a favourite spot of one of Garhwal's earliest British Commissioners, J.H. Batten, whose administration continued for twenty years (1836-56). He wrote:

> The day I reached there, it was snowing and young trees were laid prostrate under the weight of snow; the lake was frozen over to a depth of about two inches. There was no human habitation, and the place looked a veritable wilderness. The next morning when the sun appeared, the Chaukhamba and many other peaks extending as far as Kedarnath seemed covered with a new quilt of snow, as if close at hand. The whole scene was so exquisite that one could not tire of gazing at it for hours. I think a person who has a subdued settled despair in his mind would all of a sudden feel a kind of bounding and exalting cheerfulness which will be imparted to his frame by the atmosphere of Duiri Tal.

This feeling of uplift can be experienced almost anywhere along the Tungnath range. Duiri Tal is still some way off the beaten track, and anyone wishing to spend the night there should carry a tent; but further along this range, the road ascends to Dugalbeta (at about 9,000 feet) where a PWD rest-house, gaily painted, has come up like some exotic orchid in the midst of a lush meadow topped by excelsia pines and pencil cedars. Many an official who has stayed here has rhapsodised on the charms of Dugalbeta; and if you are unofficial (and therefore not entitled to stay in the bungalow), you can move on to Chopta, lusher still, where there is accommodation of a sort for pilgrims and other hardy souls. Two or three little tea-shops provide mattresses and quilts. The Garhwal Mandal is putting up a rest-house. These tourist rest-houses of Garhwal are a great boon to the traveller; but during the pilgrim season (May/June) they are filled to overflowing, and if you turn up unexpectedly you might have to take your pick of tea-shop or 'dharamshala': something of a lucky dip, since they vary a good deal in comfort and cleanliness.

The trek from Chopta to Tungnath is only three and a half miles, but in that distance one ascends about 3,000 feet, and the pilgrim may be forgiven for feeling that at places he is on a perpendicular path. Like a ladder to heaven, I couldn't help thinking.

In spite of its steepness, my companion, the redoubtable Ganesh Saili, insisted that we take a shortcut. After clawing our way up tufts of alpine grass, which formed the rungs of our ladder, we were stuck and had to inch our way down again;

so that the ascent of Tungnath began to resemble a game of Snakes and Ladders.

A tiny guardian-temple dedicated to the god Ganesh spurred us on. Nor was I really fatigued; for the cold fresh air and the verdant greenery surrounding us was like an intoxicant. Myriads of wildflowers grow on the open slopes—buttercups, anemones, wild strawberries, forget-me-not, rock-cress—enough to rival Bhyundar's 'Valley of Flowers' at this time of the year.

But before reaching these alpine meadows, we climb through rhododendron forest, and here one finds at least three species of this flower: the red-flowering tree rhododendron (found throughout the Himalaya between 6,000 feet and 10,000 feet); a second variety, the almatta, with flowers that are light red or rosy in colour; and the third chimul or white variety, found at heights ranging from between 10,000 and 13,000 feet. The chimul is a brush-wood, seldom more than twelve feet high and growing slantingly due to the heavy burden of snow it has to carry for almost six months in the year.

These brushwood rhododendrons are the last trees we see on our ascent, for as we approach Tungnath the tree line ends and there is nothing between earth and sky except grass and rock and tiny flowers. Above us, a couple of crows dive-bomb a hawk, who does his best to escape their attentions. Crows are the world's great survivors. They are capable of living at any height and in any climate; as much at home in the back streets of Delhi as on the heights of Tungnath.

Another survivor up here at any rate, is the pika, a sort of mouse-hare, who looks like neither mouse nor hare but rather a tiny guinea-pig—small ears, no tail, grey-brown fur, and chubby feet. They emerge from their holes under the rocks to forage for grasses on which to feed. Their simple diet and thick fur enable them to live in extreme cold, and they have been found at 16,000 feet, which is higher than any other mammal lives. The Garhwalis call this little creature the runda—at any rate, that's what the temple priest called it, adding that it was not averse to entering houses and helping itself to grain and other delicacies. So perhaps there's more in it of mouse than of hare.

These little rundas were with us all the way from Chopta to Tungnath; peering out from their rocks or scampering about on the hillside, seemingly unconcerned by our presence. At Tungnath' they live beneath the temple flagstones. The priest's grandchildren were having a game discovering their burrows; the rundas would go in at one hole and pop out at another—they must have had a system of underground passages.

When we arrived, clouds had gathered over Tungnath, as they do almost every afternoon. The temple looked austere in the gathering gloom.

To some, the name 'tung' indicates 'lofty', from the position of the temple on the highest peak outside the main chain of the Himalaya; others derive it from the word 'tunga', that is 'to be suspended'—an allusion to the form under which the deity is worshipped here. The form is the Swayambhu Ling. On Shivratri or Night of Shiva, the true believer may, 'with the eye of faith', see the lingam increase in size; but 'to the evil-minded no such favour is granted'.

The temple, though not very large, is certainly impressive, mainly because of its setting and the solid slabs of grey granite from which it is built. The whole place somehow puts me in mind of Emily Bronte's *Wuthering Heights*—bleak, windswept, open to the skies. And as you look down from the temple at the little half-deserted hamlet that serves it in summer, the eye is met by grey slate roofs and piles of stones, with just a few hardy souls in residence—for the majority of pilgrims now prefer to spend the night down at Chopta.

Even the temple priest, attended by his son and grandsons, complains bitterly of the cold. To spend every day barefoot on those cold flagstones must indeed be hardship. I wince after five minutes of it, made worse by stepping into a puddle of icy water. I shall never make a good pilgrim; no rewards for me, in this world or the next. But the pandit's feet are literally thick-skinned; and the children seem oblivious to the cold. Still in October they must be happy to descend to Maku, their home village on the slopes below Dugalbeta.

It begins to rain as we leave the temple. We pass herds of sheep huddled in a ruined dharamshala. The crows are still rushing about the grey weeping skies, although the hawk has very sensibly gone away. A runda sticks his nose out from his hole, probably to take a look at the weather. There is a clap of thunder and he disappears, like the white rabbit in *Alice in Wonderland*. We are halfway down the Tungnath 'ladder' when it begins to rain quite heavily. And now we pass our first genuine pilgrims, a group of intrepid Bengalis who are heading straight into the storm. They are without umbrellas or raincoats, but they are not to be deterred. Oaks and rhododendrons flash past as we dash down the steep, winding path. Another short cut, and Ganesh Saili takes a tumble, but is cushioned by moss and buttercups. My wrist-watch strikes a rock and the glass is shattered. No matter. Time here is of little or no consequence. Away with time! Is this, I wonder, the 'bounding and exalting cheerfulness' experienced by Batten and now manifesting itself in me?

The tea-shop beckons. How would one manage in the hills without these wayside tea-shops? Miniature inns, they provide food, shelter and even lodging to dozens at a time. We sit on a bench between a Gujar herdsman and a pilgrim who is too feverish to make the climb to the temple. He accepts my offer of an aspirin to go with his tea. We tackle some buns—rock-hard, to match our environment—and wash the pellets down with hot sweet tea.

There is a small shrine here, too, right in front of the tea-shop. It is a slab of rock roughly shaped like a lingam, and it is daubed with vermilion and strewn with offerings of wildflowers. The mica in the rock gives it a beautiful sheen.

I suppose Hinduism comes closest to being a nature religion. Rivers, rocks, trees, plants, animals and birds, all play their part, both in mythology and in everyday worship. This harmony is most evident in these remote places, where gods and mountains co-exist. Tungnath, as yet unspoilt by a materialistic society, exerts its magic on all who come here with open mind and heart.

SEVEN

Trees by My Window

Living at seven thousand feet, I am fortunate to have a big window that opens out on the forest so that the trees are almost within my reach. If I jumped, I could land quite neatly in the arms of an oak or horse chestnut. I have never made that leap, but the big langurs—silver-gray monkeys with long, swishing tails—often spring from the trees onto my corrugated tin roof, making enough noise to frighten all the birds away.

Standing on its own outside my window is a walnut tree, and truly this is a tree for all seasons. In winter the branches are bare, but beautifully smooth and rounded. In spring each limb produces a bright green spear of new growth, and by mid-summer the entire tree is in leaf. Toward the end of the monsoon the walnuts, encased in their green jackets, have reached maturity. When the jackets begin to split, you can see the hard brown shells of the nuts, and inside each shell is the delicious meat itself.

Every year this tree gives me a basket of walnuts. But last year the nuts were disappearing one by one, and I was at a loss as to who had been taking them. Could it have been the milkman's small son? He was an inveterate tree climber, but he was usually to be found on the oak trees, gathering fodder for his herd. He admitted that his cows had enjoyed my dahlias, which they had eaten the previous week, but he stoutly denied having fed them walnuts.

It wasn't the woodpecker either. He was out there every day, knocking furiously against the bark of the tree, trying to pry an insect out of a narrow crack, but he was strictly non-vegetarian. As for the langurs, they ate my geraniums but did not care for the walnuts.

The nuts seemed to disappear early in the morning while I was still in bed, so one day I surprised everyone, including myself, by getting up before sunrise. I was just in time to catch the culprit climbing out of the walnut tree. She was an old woman who sometimes came to cut grass on the hillside. Her face was as wrinkled as the walnuts she so fancied, but her arms and legs were very sturdy.

'And how many walnuts did you gather today, Grandmother?' I asked.

'Just two,' she said with a giggle, offering them to me on her open palm. I accepted one, and thus encouraged, she climbed higher into the tree and helped herself to the remaining nuts. It was impossible for me to object. I was taken with admiration for her agility. She must have been twice my age, but I knew I could never get up that tree. To the victor, the spoils!

Unlike the prized walnuts, the horse chestnuts are inedible. Even the rhesus monkeys throw them away in disgust. But the tree itself is a friendly one, especially in summer when it is in full leaf. The lightest breeze makes the leaves break into conversation, and their rustle is a cheerful sound. The spring flowers of the horse chestnut look like candelabra, and when the blossoms fall, they carpet the hillside with their pale pink petals.

Another of my favorites is the deodar. It stands erect and dignified and does not bend with the wind. In spring the new leaves, or needles, are a tender green, while during the monsoon the tiny young cones spread like blossoms in the dark green folds of the branches. The deodar enjoys the company of its own kind: where one deodar grows, there will be others. A walk in a deodar forest is awe-inspiring—surrounded on all sides by these great sentinels of the mountains, you feel as though the trees themselves are on the march.

I walk among the trees outside my window often, acknowledging their presence with a touch of my hand against their trunks. The oak has been there the longest, and the wind has bent its upper branches and twisted a few so that it looks shaggy and undistinguished. But it is a good tree for the privacy of birds. Sometimes it seems completely uninhabited

until there is a whirring sound, as of a helicopter approaching, and a party of long-tailed blue magpies flies across the forest glade.

Most of the pines near my home are on the next hillside. But there is a small Himalayan blue a little way below the cottage, and sometimes I sit beneath it to listen to the wind playing softly in its branches.

When I open the window at night, there is almost always something to listen to: the mellow whistle of a pygmy owlet, or the sharp cry of a barking deer. Sometimes, if I am lucky, I will see the moon coming up over the next mountain, and two distant deodars in perfect silhouette.

Some night sounds outside my window remain strange and mysterious. Perhaps they are the sounds of the trees themselves, stretching their limbs in the dark, shifting a little, flexing their fingers, whispering to one another. These great trees of the mountains, I feel they know me well, as I watch them and listen to their secrets, happy to rest my head beneath their outstretched arms.

EIGHT

'Let's Go to the Pictures!'

My love affair with the cinema began when I was five and ended when I was about fifty. Not because I wanted it to, but because all my favourite cinema halls were closing down—being turned into shopping malls or garages or just disappearing altogether.

There was something magical about sitting in a darkened cinema hall, the audience silent, completely focused on the drama unfolding on the big screen. You could escape to a different world—run away to Dover with David Copperfield, sail away to a treasure island with Long John Silver, dance the light fantastic with Fred Astaire or Gene Kelly, sing with Saigal or Deanna Durbin or Nelson Eddy, fall in love with Madhubala or Elizabeth Taylor. And until the lights came on at the end of the show you were in their world, far removed from the troubles of one's own childhood or the struggles of early manhood.

Watching films on TV cannot be the same. People come and go, the power comes and goes, other viewers keep switching the channels, food is continually being served or consumed, family squabbles are ever present, and there is no escape from those dreaded commercials that are repeated every ten or fifteen minutes or even between overs if you happen to be watching cricket.

No longer do we hear that evocative suggestion: 'Let's go to the pictures!'

Living in Mussoorie where there are no longer any functioning cinemas, the invitation is heard no more. I'm afraid there isn't half as much excitement in the words 'Let's put on the TV!'

For one thing, going to the pictures meant going out—on foot, or on a bicycle, or in the family car. When I lived on the outskirts of Mussoorie it took me almost an hour to climb the hill into town to see a film at one of our tiny halls—but walk I did, in hot sun or drenching rain or icy wind, because going to the pictures was an event in itself, a break from more mundane activities, quite often a social occasion. You would meet friends from other parts of the town, and after the show you would join them in a cafe for a cup of tea and the latest gossip. A stroll along the Mall and a visit to the local bookshop would bring the evening to a satisfying end. A long walk home under the stars, a drink before dinner, something to listen to on the radio ... 'And then to bed,' as Mr Pepys would have said.

Not that everything went smoothly in our small-town cinemas. In Shimla, Mussoorie and other hill-stations, the roofs were of corrugated tin sheets, and when there was heavy rain or a hailstorm it would be impossible to hear the sound-track. You had then to imagine that you were back in the silent film era.

Mussoorie's oldest cinema, the Picture Palace, did in fact open early in the silent era. This was in 1912, the year electricity came to the town. Later, its basement floor was also turned into a cinema, the Jubilee, which probably made it India's first multiplex hall. Sadly, both closed down about five years ago, along with the Rialto, the Majestic and the Capitol (below Halman's Hotel).

In Shimla, we had the Ritz, the Regal and the Rivoli. This was when I was a schoolboy at Bishop Cotton's. How we used to look forward to our summer and autumn breaks. We would be allowed into town during these holidays, and we lost no time in tramping up to the Ridge to take in the latest films. Sometimes we'd arrive wet or perspiring, but the changeable weather did not prevent us from enjoying the film. One-and-a-half hours escape from the routine and discipline of boarding school life. Fast foods had yet to be invented, but roasted peanuts or *bhuttas* would keep us going. They were cheap too. The cinema ticket was just over a rupee. If you had five rupees in your pocket you could enjoy a pleasant few hours in the town.

It was during the winter holidays—three months of time on my hands—that I really caught up with the films of the day.

New Delhi, the winter of 1943. World War II was still in progress. The halls were flooded with British and American movies. My father would return from Air Headquarters, where he'd been working on cyphers all day. 'Let's go to the pictures' he'd say, and we'd be off to the Regal or Rivoli or Odeon or Plaza, only a short walk from our rooms on Atul Grove Road.

Comedies were my favourites. Laurel and Hardy, Abbot and Costello, George Formby, Harold Lloyd, the Marx Brothers.... And sometimes we'd venture further afield, to the old Ritz at Kashmere Gate, to see Sabu in *The Thief of Baghdad* or *Cobra Woman*. These Arabian Nights-type entertainments were popular in the old city.

The *Statesman*, the premier newspaper of that era, ran ads for all the films in town, and I'd cut them out and stick them in a scrapbook. I could rattle off the cast of all the pictures I'd seen, and today, sixty years later, I can still name all the actors (and sometimes the director) of almost every 1940's film.

My father died when I was ten and I went to live with my mother and stepfather in Dehra Dun. Dehra too, was well served with cinemas, but I was a lonely picturegoer. I had no friends or companions in those years, and I would trudge off on my own to the Orient or Odeon or Hollywood, to indulge in a few hours of escapism. Books were there, of course, providing another and better form of escape, but books had to be read in the home, and sometimes I wanted to get away from the house and pursue a solitary other-life in the anonymous privacy of a darkened cinema hall.

It has gone now, the little Odeon cinema opposite the old Parade Ground in Dehra. Many of my age, and younger, will remember it with affection, for it was probably the most popular meeting place for English cinema buffs in the '40s and '50s. You could get a good idea of the popularity of a film by looking at the number of bicycles ranged outside. Dehra was a bicycle town. The scooter hadn't been invented, and cars were few. I belonged to a minority of walkers. I have walked all over the towns and cities I have lived in—Dehradun, New and Old Delhi, London, St Helier (in Jersey), and our hill-stations. Those walks often ended at the cinema!

The Odeon was a twenty-minute walk from the Old Survey Road, where we lived at the time, and after the evening show I would walk home across the deserted parade ground, the starry night adding to my dreams of a starry world, where tap-dancers, singing cowboys, swashbuckling swordsmen, and glamorous women in sarongs reigned supreme in the firmament. I wasn't just a daydreamer; I was a star-dreamer.

During the intervals (five-minute breaks between the shorts and the main feature), the projectionist or his assistant would play a couple of gramophone records for the benefit of the audience. Unfortunately the management had only two or three records, and the audience would grow restless listening to the same tunes at every show. I must have been compelled to listed to *Don't Fence Me In* about a hundred times, and felt thoroughly fenced in.

At home I had a good collection of gramophone records, passed on to me by relatives and neighbours who were leaving India around the time of Independence. I decided it would be a good idea to give some of them to the cinema's management so that we could be provided with a little more variety during the intervals. I made a selection of about twenty records— mostly dance music of the period—and presented them to the manager, Mr Suri.

Mr Suri was delighted. And to show me his gratitude, he presented me with a Free Pass which permitted me to see all the pictures I liked without having to buy a ticket! Any day, any show, for as long as Mr Suri was the manager! Could any ardent picturegoer have asked for more?

This unexpected bonanza lasted for almost two years with the result that during my school holidays I saw a film every second day. Two days was the average run for most films. Except *Gone With the Wind*, which ran for a week, to my great chagrin. I found it so boring that I left in the middle.

Usually I did enjoy films based on famous or familiar books. Dickens was a natural for the screen. *David Copperfield*, *Oliver Twist*, *Great Expectations*, *Nicholas Nickleby*, *A Tale of Two Cities*,

Pickwick Papers, *A Christmas Carol* (Scrooge) all made successful films, true to the originals. Daphne du Maurier's novels also transferred well to the screen. As did Somerset Maugham's works: *Of Human Bondage*, *The Razor's Edge*, *The Letter*, *Rain* and several others.

Occasionally I brought the management a change of records. Mr Suri was not a very communicative man, but I think he liked me (he knew something about my circumstances) and with a smile and a wave of the hand he would indicate that the freedom of the hall was mine.

Eventually, school finished, I was packed off to England, where my picture-going days went into a slight decline. No Free Passes any more. But on Jersey island, where I lived and worked for a year, I found an out-of-the-way cinema which specialised in showing old comedies, and here I caught up with many British film comedians such as Tommy Trinder, Sidney Howard, Max Miller, Will Hay, Old Mother Riley (a man in reality) and Gracie Fields. These artistes had been but names to me, as their films had never come to India. I was thrilled to be able to discover and enjoy their considerable talents. You would be hard put to find their films today; they have seldom been revived.

In London for two years I had an office job and most of my spare time was spent in writing (and rewriting) my first novel. All the same, I took to the streets and discovered the Everyman cinema in Hampstead, which showed old classics,

including the films of Jean Renoir and Orson Welles. And the
Academy in Leicester Square, which showed the best films from
the continent. I also discovered a couple of seedy litte cinemas
in the East End, which appropriately showed the early gangster
films of James Cagney and Humphrey Bogart.

I also saw the first Indian film to get a regular screening
in London. It was called *Aan*, and was the usual extravagant
mix of music and melodrama. But it ran for two or three weeks.
Homesick Indians (which included me) flocked to see it. One
of its stars was Nadira, who specialised in playing the scheming
sultry villainess. A few years ago she came out of retirement
to take the part of Miss Mackenzie in a TV serial based on some
of my short stories set in Mussoorie. A sympathetic role for
a change. And she played it to perfection.

It was four years before I saw Dehra again. Mr Suri had gone
elsewhere. The little cinema had closed down and was about
to be demolished, to make way for a hotel and a block of shops.

We must move on, of course. There's no point in hankering
after distant pleasures and lost picture palaces. But there's no
harm in indulging in a little nostalgia. What is nostalgia, after
all, but an attempt to preserve that which was good in the past?

And last year I was reminded of that golden era of the silver
screen. I was rummaging around in a *kabari* shop in one of

Dehradun's bazaars where I came across a pile of old 78 rpm records, all looking a little the worse for wear. And on a couple of them I found my name scratched on the labels. *Pennies from Heaven* was the title of one of the songs. It had certainly saved me a few rupees. That and the goodwill of Mr Suri, the Odeon's manager, all those years ago.

I bought the records. Can't play them now. No wind-up gramophone! But I am a sentimental fellow and I keep them among my souvenirs as a reminder of the days when I walked home alone across the silent, moonlit parade ground, after the evening show was over.

NINE

Some Hill-Station Ghosts

Shimla has its phantom rickshaw and Lansdowne its headless horseman. Mussoorie has its woman in white. Late at night, she can be seen sitting on the parapet wall on the winding road up to the hill-station. Don't stop to offer her a lift. She will fix you with her evil eye and ruin your holiday.

The Mussoorie taxi drivers and other locals call her Bhoot-Aunty. Everyone has seen her at some time or the other. To give her a lift is to court disaster. Many accidents have been attributed to her baleful presence. And when people pick themselves up from the road (or are picked up by concerned citizens), Bhoot-Aunty is nowhere to be seen, although survivors swear that she was in the car with them.

Ganesh Saili, Abha and I were coming back from Dehra Dun late one night when we saw this woman in white sitting on the parapet by the side of the road. As our headlights fell on her, she turned her face away, Ganesh, being a thorough gentleman, slowed down and offered her a lift. She turned towards us then, and smiled a wicked smile. She seemed quite attractive except that her canines protruded slightly in vampire fashion.

'Don't stop!' screamed Abha. 'Don't even look at her! It's Bhoot-Aunty!'

Ganesh pressed down on the accelerator and sped past her. Next day we heard that a tourist's car had gone off the road and the occupants had been severely injured. The accident took place shortly after they had stopped to pick up a woman in white who had wanted a lift. But she was not among the injured.

Miss Ripley-Bean, an old English lady who was my neighbour when I lived near Wynberg-Allen school, told me that her family was haunted by a malignant phantom head that always appeared before the death of one of her relatives.

She said her brother saw this apparition the night before her mother died, and both she and her sister saw it before the death of their father. The sister slept in the same room. They were both awakened one night by a curious noise in the cupboard facing their beds. One of them began getting out of bed to see if their cat was in the room, when the cupboard door suddenly opened and a luminous head appeared. It was

covered with matted hair and appeared to be in an advanced stage of decomposition. Its fleshless mouth grinned at the terrified sisters. And then as they crossed themselves, it vanished.

The next day they learned that their father, who was in Lucknow, had died suddenly, at about the time that they had seen the death's head.

Everyone likes to hear stories about haunted houses; even sceptics will listen to a ghost story, while casting doubts on its veracity.

Rudyard Kipling wrote a number of memorable ghost stories set in India—*Imray's Return, The Phantom Rickshaw, The Mark of the Beast, The End of the Passage*—his favorite milieu being the haunted *dak* bungalow. But it was only after his return to England that he found himself actually having to live in a haunted house. He writes about it in his autobiography, *Something of Myself*:

> The spring of '96 saw us in Torquay, where we found a house for our heads that seemed almost too good to be true. It was large and bright, with big rooms each and all open to the sun, the ground embellished with great trees and the warm land dipping southerly to the clean sea under the Mary Church cliffs. It had been inhabited for thirty years by three old maids.

The revelation came in the shape of a growing depression which enveloped us both—a gathering blackness of mind and sorrow of the heart, that each put down to the new, soft climate and, without telling the other, fought against for long weeks. It was the Feng-shui—the Spirit of the house itself—that darkened the sunshine and fell upon us every time we entered, checking the very words on our lips.... We paid forfeit and fled. More than thirty years later we returned down the steep little road to that house, and found, quite unchanged, the same brooding spirit of deep despondency within the rooms.

Again, thirty years later, he returned to this house in his short story, 'The House Surgeon,' in which two sisters cannot come to terms with the suicide of a third sister, and brood upon the tragedy day and night until their thoughts saturate every room of the house.

Many years ago, I had a similar experience in a house in Dehra Dun, in which an elderly English couple had died from neglect and starvation. In 1947, when many European residents were leaving the town and emigrating to the UK, this poverty-stricken old couple, sick and friendless, had been forgotten. Too ill to go out for food or medicine, they had died in their beds, where they were discovered several days later by the landlord's munshi.

The house stood empty for several years. No one wanted to live in it. As a young man, I would sometimes roam about the neglected grounds or explore the cold, bare rooms, now stripped of furniture, doorless and windowless, and I would be assailed by a feeling of deep gloom and depression. Of course I knew what had happened there, and that may have contributed to the effect the place had on me. But when I took a friend, Jai Shankar, through the house, he told me he felt quite sick with apprehension and fear. 'Ruskin, why have you brought me to this awful house?' he said. 'I'm sure it's haunted.' And only then did I tell him about the tragedy that had taken place within its walls.

Today, the house is used as a government office. No one lives in it at night except for a Gurkha *chowkidar*, a man of strong nerves who sleeps in the back verandah. The atmosphere of the place doesn't bother him, but he does hear strange sounds in the night. 'Like someone crawling about on the floor above,' he tells me. 'And someone groaning. These old houses are noisy places...'

A morgue is not a noisy place, as a rule. And for a morgue attendant, corpses are silent companions.

Old Mr Jacob, who lives just behind the cottage, was once a morgue attendant for the local mission hospital. In those days it was situated at Sunny Bank, about a hundred metres up the hill from here. One of the outhouses served as the morgue: Mr Jacob begs me not to identify it.

He tells me of a terrifying experience he went through when he was doing night duty at the morgue.

'The body of a young man was found floating in the Aglar river, behind Landour, and was brought to the morgue while I was on night duty. It was placed on the table and covered with a sheet.

'I was quite accustomed to seeing corpses of various kinds and did not mind sharing the same room with them, even after dark. On this occasion a friend had promised to join me, and to pass the time I strolled around the room, whistling a popular tune. I think it was "Danny Boy," if I remember right. My friend was a long time coming, and I soon got tired of whistling and sat down on the bench beside the table. The night was very still, and I began to feel uneasy. My thoughts went to the boy who had drowned and I wondered what he had been like when he was alive. Dead bodies are so impersonal...

'The morgue had no electricity, just a kerosene lamp, and after some time I noticed that the flame was very low. As I was about to turn it up, it suddenly went out. I lit the lamp again, after extending the wick. I returned to the bench, but I had not been sitting there for long when the lamp again went out, and something moved very softly and quietly past me.

'I felt quite sick and faint, and could hear my heart pounding away. The strength had gone out of my legs, otherwise I would have fled from the room. I felt quite weak and helpless, unable even to call out....

'Presently the footsteps came nearer and nearer. Something cold and icy touched one of my hands and felt its way up towards my neck and throat. It was behind me, then it was before me. Then it was *over* me. I was in the arms of the corpse!

'I must have fainted, because when I woke up I was on the floor, and my friend was trying to revive me. The corpse was back on the table.'

'It may have been a nightmare,' I suggested 'Or you allowed your imagination to run riot.'

'No,' said Mr Jacobs. 'There were wet, slimy marks on my clothes. And the feet of the corpse matched the wet footprints on the floor.'

After this experience, Mr Jacobs refused to do any more night duty at the morgue.

A Chakrata Haunting

From Herbertpur near Paonta you can go up to Kalsi, and then up the hill road to Chakrata.

Chakrata is in a security zone, most of it off limits to tourists, which is one reason why it has remained unchanged in 150 years of its existence. This small town's population of 1,500 is the same today as it was in 1947—probably the only town in India that hasn't shown a population increase.

Courtesy a government official, I was fortunate enough to be able to stay in the forest rest-house on the outskirts of the town. This is a new building, the old rest-house—a little way downhill—having fallen into disuse. The chowkidar told me the old rest-house was haunted, and that this was the real reason for its having been abandoned. I was a bit sceptical about this, and asked him what kind of haunting took place in it. He told me that he had himself gone through a frightening experience in the old house, when he had gone there to light a fire for some forest officers who were expected that night. After lighting the fire, he looked round and saw a large black animal, like a wild cat, sitting on the wooden floor and gazing into the fire. 'I called out to it, thinking it was someone's pet. The creature turned, and looked full at me with *eyes that were human*, and a face which was the *face of an ugly woman*! The creature snarled at me, and the snarl became an angry howl. Then it vanished!'

'And what did you do?' I asked.

'I vanished too,' said the chowkidar. I haven't been down to that house again.'

I did not volunteer to sleep in the old house but made myself comfortable in the new one, where I hoped I would not be troubled by any phantom. However, a large rat kept me company, gnawing away at the woodwork of a chest of drawers. Whenever I switched on the light it would be silent, but as soon as the light was off, it would start gnawing away again.

This reminded me of a story old Miss Kellner (of my Dehra childhood) told me, of a young man who was desperately in love with a girl who did not care for him. One day, when he was following her in the street, she turned on him and, pointing to a rat which some boys had just killed, said, 'I'd as soon marry that rat as marry you.' He took her cruel words so much to heart that he pined away and died. After his death the girl was haunted at night by a rat and occasionally she would be bitten. When the family decided to emigrate they travelled down to Bombay in order to embark on a ship sailing for London. The ship had just left the quay, when shouts and screams were heard from the pier. The crowd scattered, and a huge rat with fiery eyes ran down to the end of the quay. It sat there, screaming with rage, then jumped into the water and disappeared. After that (according to Miss Kellner), the girl was not haunted again.

Old dak bungalows and forest rest houses have a reputation for being haunted. And most hill-stations have their resident ghosts—and ghost writers! But I will not extend this catalogue of ghostly hauntings and visitations, as I do not want to discourage tourists from visiting Landour and Mussoorie. In some countries, ghosts are an added attraction for tourists. Britain boasts of hundreds of haunted castles and stately homes, and visitors to Romania seek out Transylvania and Dracula's castle. So do we promote Bhoot-Aunty as a tourist attraction? Only if she reforms and stops sending vehicles off those hairpin bends that lead to Mussoorie.

TEN

The Year of the Kissing and Other Good Times

'Seeds of the potato-berries should be sown in adapted places by explorers of new countries.'

So declared a botanically-minded empire-builder. And among those who took this advice was Captain Young of the Sirmur Rifles, Commandant of the Doon from the end of the Gurkha War in 1815 to the time of the Mutiny (1857).

It has to be said that the good captain was motivated by self-interest. He was an Irishman and fond of potatoes. He liked his Irish stew. So he grew his own potatoes and encouraged the good people of Garhwal to grow them too. In 1823 he received a supply of superior Irish potatoes and was considering where to plant them. The northern hill districts had been in British hands for almost ten years, but as yet no one had thought of resorting to them for rest or relaxation. The hills of central India, covered with jungle, were known to be extremely unhealthy. The Siwaliks near Dehradun were malarious. It was supposed that the Himalayan foothills, also forest clad, would be equally unhealthy. But Captain Young was to discover otherwise.

Carrying his beloved Irish potatoes with him, Captain Young set out on foot and soon left the sub-tropical Doon behind him. Above 4,000 feet he came to forests of oak and rhododendron, and above 6,000 feet they found cedars, known in the Himalayas as deodars or *devdars*—trees of the gods. He found a climate so cool and delightful that not only did he plant potatoes, he built himself a small hunting lodge facing the snows.

Captain Young was to make a number of visits to his little hut on the mountain. No one lived nearby. The villages were situated in the valleys, where water was available. Bears, leopards and wild boar roamed the forests. There were pheasants in the shady ravines and small trout in the little Aglar river. Young and his companions could hunt and fish to their hearts content. In 1826 Young, now a colonel, built the first large house, 'Mullingar' (I see its remnants from my window every morning), on the way up to what became the convalescent depot and cantonment. Others soon began to follow Young's example, settling as far away as Cloud End and The Abbey. By 1830, the twin hill-stations of Landour and Mussoorie had come into being.

Those early pleasure-seeking residents took little or no interest in potato growing, but Young certainly did, and the

of such a state of society at Home? But this was not all. 'Married ladies and married gents formed friendships and associations, which tended to no good purpose, and set a bad example.'

Adultery under the pines? Mussoorie was well ahead of the times. The poor reverend preached to no purpose. And it was just as well that he was not alive in the year 1933, when a lady stood up at a benefit show and auctioned a single kiss, for which a gentleman paid Rs 300, a substantial amount seventy years ago. (A year's house rent, in fact.) The *Statesman*'s correspondent had nothing to say on this latter occasion; his silence was in itself a comment on the changing times.

A few years ago I received a letter from a reader in England, wanting to know if there were any Maxwells still living in Mussoorie. He was a Maxwell himself, he said, by his father's first marriage. From what he knew of the family history, there ought to have been several Maxwells by the second marriage, and he wanted to get in touch with them.

He was very frank and mentioned that his father had given up a brilliant career in the Indian Civil Service to marry a fourteen-year old Muslim girl. He had met her in Madras, changed his religion to facilitate the marriage, and then—to avoid 'scandal'—had made his home with her in Mussoorie.

Although there are no longer any Maxwells living in Mussoorie, my former neighbour, Miss Bean, confirmed that Mr Maxwell's children from his second wife had grown up on

A few months later they were living in the heat and dust of Alwar, in Rajasthan, and then Jamnagar in Kathiawar, where my father conducted a small palace school. I was not born in Mussoorie but I am pretty sure I had my conception there!

There is something in the air of the place—especially in October—that is conducive to love and passion and desire. Miss Bean told me that as a girl she'd many suitors, and if she did not marry it was more from procrastination than from being passed over. While on all sides elopements and broken marriages were making hill-station life exciting, and providing orphans and illegitimate children for the mission schools, Miss Bean contrived to remain single and childless. She was probably helped by the fact of her father being a retired police officer with a reputation for being a good shot with the pistol and Lee-Enfield rifle.

She taught elocution in one of the many schools that flourished (and still flourish) in Mussoorie. There is a protective atmosphere about a residential school, an atmosphere which, although it protects one from the outside would, often exposes one to the hazards within the system.

The schools were not without their own scandals. Mrs Fennimore, the wife of a headmaster at Oak Grove, got herself entangled in a defamation suit, each hearing of which grew more and more distasteful to her husband. Unable to stand the whole weary and sordid business, Mr Fennimore hit upon a solution. Loading his revolver, he moved to his wife's bedside and shot her through the head. For no accountable reason he put the weapon under her pillow—obviously no one could have mistaken the death for suicide—and then, going to his study, he leaned over his rifle and shot himself.

Ten years later, in the same school, another headmaster's wife was arrested for attempted murder. She had fired at, and wounded a junior mistress. The motive remained obscure and the case was hushed up.

In the St. Fidelis' School, circa 1941, a boy asleep in the dormitory had his throat slit by another boy, it was said at the instigation of one of the teachers. This too was hushed up, but the school closed down a year later.

In recent years, there has been a suicide in one public school, and murders (involving students) in two others; also an accidental death by way of a drug overdose. Tom Brown's school days were pretty dull when compared to the goings-on in some of our residential schools.

These affairs usually get hushed up, but there was no hushing up the incidents that took place on the 25th July 1927, at the height of the season and in the heart of the town—a double tragedy that set the station agog with excitement. It all happened in broad daylight and in a full boarding-house, Zephyr Hall.

Shortly after noon the boarders were startled into brisk activity when a shot rang out from one of the rooms, followed by screams. Other shots followed in quick succession. Those boarders who happened to be in the lounge or on the verandah dived for the safety of their own rooms and bolted the doors. One unhappy boarder however, ignorant of where the man with the gun might be, decided to take no chances and came round the corner with his hands held well above his head— only to run straight into the levelled pistol! Even the man who held it, and who had just shot his wife and daughter, couldn't help laughing.

Mr Owen, the maniac with gun, after killing his wife and wounding his daughter finally shot himself. His was the first official Christian cremation in Mussoorie, performed apparently in compliance with wishes expressed long before his dramatic end.

A couple of years ago I had a letter from an old Mussoorie resident, Col. Cole, now retired in Pune, who recalled the event: 'Mrs Owen ran Zephyr Hall as a boarding-house. It was the last Saturday of the month, and Mrs Owen's son Basil was with me at the 11am—1 pm session at the skating rink and so escaped the tragedy that took place about mid-day, when Mr Owen shot Mrs Owen and one daughter and then shot himself. I do not know what happened to Basil but he was withdrawn from school and an uncle took him over. This was not the end of the family tragedy. An older sister of Basil's in her early twenties was boating on the river Gumpti at Lucknow with her fiance, when a flash flood took place and the strong current drowned them both.'

This was not the end of the story, at least not for me.

A few summers ago, while I was walking along the Mall, I was stopped by a stranger, a small man with pale blue eyes and thinning hair. He must have been over sixty. Accompanying him was a much younger woman, whom he introduced as his wife. He apologized for detaining me, and said: 'You look as though you have been here a long time. Do you know if any of the Gantzers still live here? I believe they look often the cemetery.'

I gave him the necessary directions and then asked him if he was visiting Mussoorie for the first time. He seemed to welcome the inquiry and showed a willingness to talk.

'It's well over fifty years since I was last here', he said. 'I was just a boy at the time'. And he gestured towards the ruins of Zephyr Hall, now occupied by postmen and their families. 'That was my mother's boarding-house. That was where she died....'

'Not—not Mr Owen?' I ventured to ask.

'That's right. So you've heard about it. My father had a sudden brainstorm. He shot and killed Mother. My sister was badly wounded. I was out at the time. Now I have come to revisit her grave. I know she'd have wanted me to come.'

He took my telephone number and promised to look me up before he left Mussoorie. But I did not see him again. After a few days, I began to wonder if I had really met a survivor of this old tragedy, or if he had been just another of the hill-station's ghosts. But one day, while I was walking along the cemetery's lowest terrace, I found confirmation that Mrs Owen's son had indeed visited his mother's grave. Set into the tombstone was a new stone plaque with the inscription: *'Mother Dear, I am Here.'*

ELEVEN

Running for Cover

The right to privacy is a fine concept and might actually work in the West, but in Eastern lands it is purely notional. If I want to be left alone, I have to be a shameless liar—pretend that I am out of town or, if that doesn't work, announce that I have measles, mumps or some new variety of Asian 'flu.

Now I happen to like people and I like meeting people from all walks of life. If this were not the case, I would have nothing to write about. But I don't like too many people all at once. They tend to get in the way. And if they arrive without warning, banging on my door while I am in the middle of composing a poem or writing a story, or simply enjoying my afternoon siesta, I am inclined to be snappy or unwelcoming. Occasionally I have even turned people away.

As I get older, that afternoon siesta becomes more of a necessity and less of an indulgence. But its strange how people love to call on me between two and four in the afternoon. I suppose it's the time of day when they have nothing to do.

'How do we get through the afternoon?' one of them will say.

'I know! Lets go and see old Ruskin. He's sure to entertain us with some stimulating conversation, if nothing else.'

Stimulating conversation in mid-afternoon? Even Socrates would have balked at it.

'I'm sorry I can't see you today,' I mutter. 'I don't feel at all well.' (In fact, extremely unwell at the prospect of several strangers gaping at me for at least half-an-hour.)

'Not well? We're so sorry. My wife here is a homeopath.'

It's amazing the number of homeopaths who turn up at my door. Unfortunately they never seem to have their little powders on them, those miracle cures for everything from headaches to hernias.

The other day a family burst in—uninvited of course. The husband was an ayurvedic physician, the wife was a homeopath (naturally), the eldest boy a medical student at an allopathic medical college.

'What do you do when one of you falls ill?' I asked, 'Do you try all three systems of medicine?'

'It depends on the ailment,' said the young man. 'But we seldom fall ill. My sister here is a yoga expert.'

His sister, a hefty girl in her late twenties (still single) looked more like an all-in wrestler than a supple yoga practitioner. She looked at my tummy. She could see I was in bad shape.

'I could teach you some exercises,' she said. 'But you'd have to come to Ludhiana.'

I felt grateful that Ludhiana was a six-hour drive from Mussoorie.

'I'll drop in some day,' I said. 'In fact, I'll come and take a course.'

We parted on excellent terms. But it doesn't always turn out that way.

There was this woman, very persistent, in fact downright rude, who wouldn't go away even when I told her I had bird-flu.

'I have to see you,' she said, 'I've written a novel, and I want you to recommend it for a Booker Prize.'

'I'm afraid I have no influence there,' I pleaded. 'I'm completely unknown in Britain.'

'Then how about the Nobel Prize?'

I thought about that for a minute. 'Only in the science field,' I said. 'If it's something to do with genes or stem cells?'

She looked at me as though I was some kind of worm. 'You are not very helpful,' she said.

'Well, let me read your book.'

'I haven't written it yet.'

'Well, why not come back when it's finished? Give yourself a year—two years—these things should never be done in a hurry.' I guided her to the gate and encouraged her down the steps.

'You are very rude,' she said. 'You did not even ask me in. I'll report you to Khushwant Singh. He's a friend of mine. He'll put you in his column.'

'If Khushwant Singh is your friend,' I said, 'why are you bothering with me? He knows all the Nobel and Booker Prize people. All the important people, in fact.'

I did not see her again, but she got my phone number from someone, and now she rings me once a week to tell me her book is coming along fine. Any day now, she's going to turn up with the manuscript.

Casual visitors who bring me their books or manuscripts are the ones I dread most. They ask me for an opinion, and if I give them a frank assessment they resent it. It's unwise to tell a would-be writer that his memoirs or novel or collected verse would be better off unpublished. Murders have been committed for less. So I play safe and say, 'Very promising. Carry on writing.' But this is fatal. Almost immediately I am asked to write a foreword or introduction, together with a letter of recommendation to my publisher—or any publisher of standing. Unwillingly I become a literacy agent; unpaid of course.

I am all for encouraging the arts and literature, but I do think writers should seek out their own publishers and write their own introductions.

The perils of doing this sort of thing was illustrated when I was prevailed upon to write a short introduction to a book about a dreaded man-eater who had taken a liking to the flesh of the good people of Dogadda, near Lansdowne. The author of the book could hardly write a decent sentence, but he managed to string together a lengthy account of the leopard's depradations. He was so persistent, calling on me or ringing me up that I finally did the introduction. He then wanted me to edit or touch up his manuscript; but this I refused to do. I would starve if I had to sit down and rewrite other people's books. But he prevailed upon me to give him a photograph.

Months later, the book appeared, printed privately of course. And there was my photograph, and a photograph of the dead leopard after it had been hunted down. But the local printer had got the captions mixed up. The dead animal's picture earned the line: 'Well-known author Ruskin Bond.' My picture carried the legend: 'Dreaded man-eater, shot after it had killed its 26th victim.'

The printer's devil had turned me into a serial killer.

Now you know why I'm wary of writing introductions.

'Vanity' publishers thrive on writers who are desperate to see their work in print. They will print and deliver a book at your doorstep and then leave you with the task of selling it; or to be more accurate, disposing of it.

One of my neighbours, Mrs Santra—may her soul rest in peace—paid a publisher forty-thousand rupees to bring out a fancy edition of her late husband's memoirs. During his lifetime he'd been unable to get it published, but before he died he got his wife to promise that she'd publish it for him. This she did, and the publisher duly delivered 500 copies to the good lady. She gave a few copies to friends, and then passed away, leaving the books behind. Her heir is now saddled with 450 hardbound volumes of unsaleable memoirs.

I have always believed that if a writer is any good he will find a publisher who will print, bind, and sell his books, and even give him a royalty for his efforts. A writer who pays to get published is inviting disappointment and heartbreak.

Many people are under the impression that I live in splendour in a large mansion, surrounded by secretaries and servants. They are disappointed to find that I live in a tiny bedroom-cum-study and that my living-room is so full of books that there is hardly space for more than three or four visitors at a time.

Sometimes thirty to forty school children turn up, wanting to see me. I don't turn away children, if I can help it. But if they come in large numbers I have to meet and talk to them on the road, which is inconvenient for everyone.

If I had the means, would I live in a splendid mansion in the more affluent parts of Mussoorie, with a film star or TV personality as my neighbour? I rather doubt it. All my life I've been living in one or two rooms and I don't think I could manage a bigger establishment. True, my extended family takes up another two rooms, but they see to it that my working space is not violated. And if I am hard at work (or fast asleep) they will try to protect me from unheralded or unwelcome visitors.

And I have learnt to tell lies. Especially when I'm asked to attend school functions as a chief guest or in some formal capacity. To spend two or three hours listening to speeches (and then being expected to give one) is my idea of hell. It's hell for the students and its hell for me. The speeches are usually followed (or preceded) by folk dances, musical interludes or class plays, and this only adds to the torment. Sports' days are just as bad. You can skip the speeches (hopefully), but you must sit out in the hot sun for the greater part of the day, while a loudspeaker informs you that little Parshottam has just broken the school record for the under-nine high jump, or that Pamela Highjinks has won the hurdles for the third year running. You don't get to see the events because you are kept busy making polite conversation with the other guests. The only occasion when a sports' event really came to life was when a misdirected discus narrowly missed decapitating the Headmaster's wife.

Former athletes and sportsmen seldom visit me. They have difficulty making it up my steps. Most of them have problems with their knees before they are fifty. They *hobble* (for want of a better word). Once their playing days are over, they start hobbling. Nandu, a former tennis champion, can't make it up my steps, nor can Chand—a former wrestler. Too much physical activity when young has resulted in an early breakdown of the body's machinery. As Nandu says, 'Body can't take it any more.' I'm not too agile either, but then, I was never much of a sportsman. Second last in the marathon was probably my most memorable achievement.

Oddly enough, some of the most frequent visitors to my humble abode are honeymooners.

Why, I don't know, but they always ask for my blessing even though I am hardly an advertisement for married bliss. A seventy-year-old bachelor blessing a newly married couple? Maybe they are under the impression that I'm a *Brahmachari*? But how would that help them? They are going to have babies sooner or later.

It is seldom that they happen to be readers or book-lovers, so why pick an author, and that too one who does not go to places of worship? However, since these young couples are inevitably attractive, and full of high hopes for their future and the future of mankind, I am happy to talk to them, wish them well…. And if it's a blessing they want, they are welcome…. My hands are far from being saintly but at least they are well-intentioned.

I have, at times, been mistaken for other people.

'Are you Mr Pickwick?' asked a small boy. At least he'd been reading Dickens. A distant relative, I said, and beamed at him in my best Pickwickian manner.

I am at ease with children, who talk quite freely except when accompanied by their parents. Then it's mum and dad who do all the talking.

'My son studies your book in school,' said one fond mother, proudly exhibiting her ten-year-old. 'He wants your autograph.'

'What's the name of the book you're reading?' I asked.

'Tom Sawyer,' he said promptly.

So I signed Mark Twain in his autograph book. He seemed quite happy.

A schoolgirl asked me to autograph her maths textbook.

'But I failed in maths,' I said. 'I'm just a story-writer.'

'How much did you get?'

'Four out of a hundred.'

She looked at me rather crossly and snatched the book away.

I have signed books in the names of Enid Blyton, R.K. Narayan, Ian Botham, Daniel Defoe, Harry Potter and the Swiss Family Robinson. No one seems to mind.

The Postman Knocks

As a freelance writer, most of my adult life has revolved around the coming of the postman. 'A cheque in the mail,' is something that every struggling writer looks forward to. It might, of course, arrive by courier, or it might not come at all. But for the most past, the acceptances and rejections of my writing life, along with editorial correspondence, readers' letters, page proofs and author's copies—how welcome they are!—come through the post.

The postman has always played a very real and important part in my life, and continues to do so. He climbs my twenty-one steps every afternoon, knocks loudly on my door—three raps, so that I know its him and not some inquisitive tourist—and gives me my registered mail or speed-post with a smile and a bit of local gossip. The gossip is important. I like to what's happening in the bazaar—who's getting married, who's standing for election, who ran away with the headmaster's wife, and whose funeral procession is passing by. He deserves a bonus for this sort of information.

The courier boy, by contrast, shouts to me from the road below and I have to go down to him. He's mortally afraid of dogs and there are three in the building. My postman isn't bothered by dogs. He comes in all weathers, and he comes on foot except when someone gives him a lift. He turns up when it's snowing, or when it's raining cats and dogs, or when there's a heat wave, and he's quite philosophical about it all. He meets all kinds of people. He has seen joy and sorrow in the homes he visits. He knows something about life. If he wasn't a philosopher to begin with, he will certainly be one by the time he retires.

Of course, not all postmen are paragons of virtue. A few years ago, we had a postman who never got further than the country liquor shop in the bazaar. The mail would pile up there for days, until he sobered up and condescended to deliver it. In due course he was banished to another route, where there were no liquor shops.

We take the postman for granted today, but there was a time, over a hundred years ago, when the carrying of the mails was a hazardous venture, and the mail-runner, or *hirkara* as he was called, had to be armed with sword or spear. Letters were carried in leather wallets on the backs of runners, who were changed at stages of eight miles. At night, the runners were accompanied by torch-bearers—in wilder parts, by drummers called *dug-dugi wallas*—to frighten away wild animals.

The tiger population was considerable at the time, and tigers were a real threat to travellers or anyone who ventured far from their town or village. Mail-runners often fell victim to man-eating tigers. The mail-runners (most of them tribals) were armed with bows and arrows, but these were seldom effective.

In the Hazaribagh district (through which the mail had to be carried, on its way from Calcutta to Allahabad) there appears to have been a concentration of man-eating tigers. There were four passes through this district, and the tigers had them well covered. Williamson, writing in 1810, tells us that the passes were so infested with tigers that the roads were almost impassible. 'Day after day, for nearly a fortnight, some of the dak people were carried off at one or other of these passes.'

In spite of these hazards, a letter sent by dak runner used to take twelve days to reach Meerut from Calcutta. It takes about the same time today, unless you use speed-post.

At up country stations the collector of Land Revenue was the Postmaster. He was given a small postal establishment, consisting of a *munshi*, a *matsaddi* or sorter, and thirty or forty runners whose pay, in 1804, was five rupees a month. The maintenance of the dak cost the government (i.e., the East India Company) twenty-five rupees a month for each stage of eight miles. Postage stamps were introduced in 1854.

My father was an enthusastic philatelist, and when I was a small boy I could sit and watch him pore over his stamp collection, which included several early and valuable Indian issues. He would grumble at the very dark and smudgy postmarks which obliterated most of Queen Victoria's profile from the stamps. This was due to the composition of the ink used for cancelling the earlier stamps. It was composed of two parts lamp-black, four parts linseed oil and three and a half of vinegar.

Letter-distributing peons, or postmen, were always smartly turned out: 'A red turban, a light green *chapkan*, a small leather belt over the breast and right shoulder, with a *chaprass* attached showing the peon's number and having the words "Post Office Peon" in English and in two vernaculars, and a bell suspended by a leather strap from the left shoulder.'

Today's postmen are more casual in their attire, although I believe they are still entitled to uniforms. The general public doesn't care how they are dressed, as long as they turn up with those letters containing *rakhis* or money orders from soldier sons and husbands. This is where the postman still scores over the fax and e-mail.

To return to our mail-runners, they were eventually replaced by the *dak-ghari* the equivalent of the English 'coach and pair'—which gradually established itself throughout the country.

A survivor into the 1940s, my Great-aunt Lillian recalled that in the late nineteenth century, before the coming of the railway, the only way of getting to Dehra Dun was by the *dak-ghari* or Night Mail. *Dak-ghari* ponies were difficult animals, she told me—'always attempting to turn around and get into the carriage with the passengers!' But once they started there was no stopping them. It was a gallop all the way to the first stage, where the ponies were changed to the accompaniment of a bugle blown by the coachman, in true Dickensian fashion.

The journey through the Siwaliks really began—as it still does—through the Mohand Pass. The ascent starts with a gradual gradient which increases as the road becomes more steep and winding. At this stage of the journey, drums were beaten (if it was day) and torches lit (if it was night) because sometimes wild elephants resented the approach of the *dak-ghari* and, trumpeting a challenge, would throw the ponies into confusion and panic, and send them racing back to the plains.

After 1900, Great-aunt Lillian used the train. But the mail bus from Saharanpur to Mussoorie still uses the old route, through the Siwaliks. And if you are lucky, you may see a herd of wild elephants crossing the road on its way to the Ganga.

And even today, in remote parts of the country, in isolated hill areas where there are no motorable roads, the mail is carried on foot, the postman often covering five or six miles every day. He never runs, true, and be might sometimes stop for a glass of tea and a game of cards en-route, but he is a reminder of those early pioneers of the postal system, the mail-runners of India.

Let me not cavil at my unexpected visitors. Sometimes they turn out to be very nice people—like the gentleman from Pune who brought me a bottle of whisky and then sat down and drank most of it himself.

TWELVE

Party Time in Mussoorie

It is very kind of people to invite me to their parties, especially as I do not throw parties myself, or invite anyone anywhere. At more than one party I have been known to throw things at people. Inspite of this—or maybe because of it—I get invited to these affairs.

I can imagine a prospective hostess saying 'Shall we invite Ruskin?'

'Would it be safe?' says her husband doubtfully. 'He has been known to throw plates at people.'

'Oh, then we *must* have him!' she shouts in glee. 'What fun it will be, watching him throw a plate at———. We'll use the cheaper crockery, of course....'

Here I am tempted to add that living in Mussoorie these forty odd years has been one long party. But if that were so, I would not be alive today. Rekha's garlic chicken and Nandu's shredded lamb would have done for me long ago. They have certainly done for my teeth. But they are only partly to blame. Hill goats are tough, stringy creatures. I remember Begum Para trying to make us rogan-josh one evening. She sat over the *degchi* for three or four hours but even then the mutton wouldn't become tender.

Begum Para, did I say?

Not *the* Begum Para? The saucy heroine of the silver screen?

And why not? This remarkable lady had dropped in from Pakistan to play the part of my grandmother in Shubhadarshini's serial *Ek Tha Rusty*, based on stores of my childhood. Not only was she a wonderful actress, she was also a wonderful person who loved cooking. But she was defeated by the Mussoorie goat, who resisted all her endeavours to turn it into an edible rogan-josh.

The Mussoorie goat is good only for getting into your garden and eating up your dahlias. These creatures also strip the hillside of any young vegetation that attempts to come up in the spring or summer. I have watched them decimate a flower garden and cause havoc to a vegetable plot. For this reason alone I do not shed a tear when I see them being marched off to the butcher's premises. I might cry over a slaughtered chicken, but not over a goat.

One of my neighbours on the hillside, Mrs K—, once kept a goat as a pet. She attempted to throw one or two parties, but no one would go to them. The goat was given the freedom of the drawing room and smelt to high heaven. Mrs K— was known to take it to bed with her. She too developed a strong odour. It is not surprising that her husband left the country and took a mistress in Panama. He couldn't get much further, poor man.

Mrs K—'s goat disappeared one day, and that same night a feast was held in Kolti village, behind Landour. People say the mutton was more tender and succulent than than at most feasts—the result, no doubt, of its having shared Mrs K—'s meals and bed for a couple of years.

One of Mrs K—'s neighbours was Mrs Santra, a kind-hearted but rather tiresome widow in her sixties. She was childless but had a fixation that, like the mother of John the Baptist, she would conceive in her sixties and give birth to a new messenger of the Messiah. Every month she would visit the local gynaecologist for advice, and the doctor would be gentle with her and tell her anything was possible and that in the meantime she should sustain herself with nourishing soups and savouries.

Mrs Santra liked giving little tea parties and I went to a couple of them. The sandwiches, samosas, cakes and jam tarts were delicious, and I expressed my appreciation. But then she took to visiting me at odd times, and I found this rather trying, as she would turn up while I was writing or sleeping or otherwise engaged. On one occasion, when I pretended I was not at home, she even followed me into the bathroom (where I had concealed myself) and scolded me for trying to avoid her.

She was a good lady, but I found it impossible to reciprocate her affectionate and even at times ardent overtures, So I had to ask her to desist from visiting me, The next day she sent her servant down with a small present—a little pot with a pansy growing in it!

On that happy note, I leave Mrs Santra and turn to other friends.

Such as Aunty Bhakti, a tremendous consumer of viands and victuals who, after a more than usually heavy meal at my former lodgings, retired to my Indian style lavatory to relieve herself. Ten minutes passed, then twenty, and still no sign of Aunty! My other luncheon guests, the Maharani Saheba of Jind, writer Bill Aitken and local *pehelwan* Maurice Alexander, grew increasingly concerned. Was Aunty having a heart attack or was she just badly constipated?

I went to the bathroom door and called out: 'Are you all right, Aunty?'

A silence, and then, in a quavering voice, 'I'm stuck!'

'Can you open the door?' I asked.

'It's open,' she said, 'but I can't move.'

I pushed open the door and peered in. Aunty, a heavily-built woman, had lost her balance and subsided backwards on the toilet, in the process jamming her bottom into the cavity!

'Give me a hand, Aunty,' I said, and taking her by the hand (the only time I'd ever been permitted to do so), tried my best to heave her out of her predicament. But she wouldn't budge.

I went back to the drawing room for help. 'Aunty's stuck,' I said, 'and I can't get her out.' The Maharani went to take a look. After all, they were cousins. She came back looking concerned. 'Bill' she said, 'get up and help Ruskin extricate Aunty before she has a heart-attack!'

Bill Aitken and I bear some resemblance to Laurel and Hardy. I'm Hardy, naturally. We did our best but Aunty Bhakti couldn't be extracted. So we called on the expertise of Maurice, our *pehelwan*, and forming a human chain or something of a tug of war team, we all pulled and tugged until Aunty Bhakti came out with a loud bang, wrecking my toilet in the process.

I must say she was not the sort to feel embarrassed. Returning to the drawing-room, she proceeded to polish off half a brick of ice-cream.

Another ice-cream fiend is Nandu Jauhar who, at the time of writing, owns the Savoy in Mussoorie. At a marriage party, and in my presence he polished off thirty-two cups of ice-cream and this after a hefty dinner.

The next morning he was as green as his favorite pistachio ice-cream.

When admonished, all he could say was 'They were only small cups, you know.'

Nandu's eating exploits go back to his schooldays when (circa 1950) he held the Doon School record for consuming the largest number of mangoes—a large bucketful, all of five kilos—in one extended sitting.

'Could you do it again?' we asked him the other day.

'Only if they are Alfonsos,' he said 'And you have to pay for them.'

Fortunately for our pockets, and for Nandu's well-being, Alfonsos are not available in Mussoorie in December.

You must meet Rekha someday. She grows herbs now, and leads the quiet life, but in her heyday she gave some memorable parties, some of them laced with a bit of pot or marijuana. Rekha was a full-blooded American girl who had married into a well-known and highly respected Brahmin family and taken an Indian name. She was highly respected too, because she'd produced triplets at her first attempt at motherhood.

Some of her old Hippie friends often turned up at her house. One of them, a French sitar player, wore a red sock on his left foot and a green sock on his right. His shoes were decorated with silver sequins. Another of her friends was an Australian film producer who had yet to produce a film. On one occasion I found the Frenchman and the Australian in Lakshmi's garden, standing in the middle of a deep hole they'd been digging.

I thought they were preparing someone's grave and asked them who it was meant for. They told me they were looking for a short cut to Australia, and carried on digging. As I never saw them again, I presume they came out in the middle of the great Australian desert. Yes, her pot was that potent!

I have never smoked pot, and have never felt any inclination to do so. One can get a great 'high' from so many other things—falling in love, or reading a beautiful poem, or taking in the perfume of a rose, or getting up at dawn to watch the morning sky and then the sunrise, or listening to great music, or just listening to bird song—it does seen rather pointless having to depend on artificial stimulants for relaxation; but human beings are a funny lot and will often go to great lengths to obtain the sort of things that some would consider rubbish.

I have no intention of adopting a patronizing, moralising tone. I did, after all, partake of Rekha's *bhang* pakoras one evening before Diwali, and I discovered a great many stars that I hadn't seen before.

I was in such high spirits that I insisted on being carried home by the two most attractive girls at the party—Abha Saili and Shenaz Kapadia—and they, having also partaken of those magical pakoras, were only too happy to oblige.

They linked arms to form a sort of chariot-seat, and I sat upon it (I was much lighter then) and was carried with great dignity and aplomb down Landour's upper Mall, stopping only now and then to remove the odd, disfiguring nameplate from an offending gate.

On our way down, we encountered a lady on her way up. Well, she looked like a lady to me, and I took off my cap and wished her good evening and asked where she was going at one o' clock in the middle of the night.

She sailed past us without deigning to reply.

'Snooty old bitch!' I called out. 'Just who is that midnight woman?' I asked Abha.

'It's not a woman,' said Abha. 'It's the circuit judge.'

'The circuit judge is taking a circuitous route home,' I commented. 'And why is he going about in drag?'

'Hush. He's not in drag. He's wearing his wig!'

'Ah well,' I said 'Even judges must have their secret vices. We must live and let live!'

They got me home in style, and I'm glad I never had to come up before the judge. He'd have given me more than a wigging.

That was a few years ago. Our Diwalis are far more respectable now, and Rekha sends us sweets instead of pakoras. But those were the days, my friend. We thought they'd never end.

In fact, they haven't. It's still party-time in Landour and Mussoorie.

★

__4 MAR 2005

Savoy Hotel

Estd. 1890

THE MALL, MUSSOORIE-248 179 UTTARANCHAL INDIA

March 1, 2005

To Whom It May Concern

This is to certify that Mr. Ruskin Bond and Mr. Ganesh Saili have supported the Savoy Bar in more ways than one during the last thirty years. They must hold a world record for never having paid for their drinks, hence I am now having to make other arrangements.

I wish them every success in their endeavours to find a new watering place.

Yours truly,
Nandu

THIRTEEN

Forward!

Of course living in Mussoorie hasn't always been fun and games. Sometimes it was a struggle to make both ends meet. Occasionally there were periods of ill-health. Friends went away. Some passed on. But looking back over the years, there is much to recall with pleasure and gratitude. Here are a few bright memories:

Nothing brighter than the rhododendrons in full bloom towards the end of March. Their scarlet blossoms bring new life to the drab winter hillside. In the plains it is the Dhak, or Flame of the Forest, that heralds the spring. Here—as in Dalhousie, Shimla, and other hill-stations—it is the tree rhododendron.

At one time picnics were very much a part of hill-station life. You packed your lunch and trudged off to some distant stream or waterfall. My most memorable princes were on Pari Tibba or at Mossy Falls, further down. Mossy Falls, I was told, was named after Mr Moss, director of the Alliance Bank. When the Bank collapsed, Mr Moss jumped off the waterfall. But there wasn't enough water in it to drown him, and inspite of his fall he lived to a ripe old age.

The years slip by and we grow old, but the days of our youth remain fresh in our minds. Like the day Sushila and I walked, or rather paddled, up the stream from above the Falls. Holding hands, partly to support each other, but mainly because we wanted to.... Her slow, enchanting smile, her long lustrous black hair, her slender feet, all remain fresh in my memory. A magical day, a magical year. And today, some forty years later, I cannot help feeling that if I go down to that stream again, I will find our footprints embedded in the sand.

Another clear memory is of my first visit to the hill-station—not just forty years ago, when I came to settle here, but *sixty-five* years ago.... A small boy of seven, I was placed in a convent school, where I was very unhappy. But my father came to see me during the summer break, and kept me with him in a boarding-house on the Mall. Always the best of companions, he took me to the pictures and for long pony and rickshaw-rides. A little cinema below Hakman's was my favourite. Hakman's was a great place then, with a band and a dance-hall and a posh restaurant. Nearby there was a skating-rink, which was consumed by a fire in the 1960s. We had no fire-engine then. We have one now, but when Victor Banerjee's house caught fire a few years ago, the fire-engine could not negotiate the narrow Landour bazaar, and by the time it arrived the house had burnt down. Victor was very philosophical about the whole thing, and went about re-building his dream house which is a great improvement on the old one.

At seventy-one (my age, not Victor's), it is time to look forward, not backward, and one should not dwell too much on the past but prepare oneself to make the most of whatever time is left to us on this fascinating planet. That is why I called my Foreword a Backward, and this epilogue a Forward—for forward we must march, whatever our age or declining physical prowess. Life has always got something new to offer.

As I write, a small white butterfly flutters in at the open window, reminding me of all that Nature offers to anyone who is receptive enough to appreciate its delights. One of my earliest stories, written over fifty years ago, was about a small yellow butterfly settling on my grandmother's knitting-needles and setting off a train of reminiscence. Now I have done with reminiscing, and this particular butterfly is here to invite me outside, to walk in the sunshine and revel in the glories of a Himalayan Spring.

The children are watching Jackie Chan on television. Their mother is cutting up beans prior to preparing lunch. Their grandmother is giving the dog a bath. These cheerful folk are members of my extended family. It's a normal day for them, and I hope it stays that way. I don't want too much excitement just now—not while I'm trying to finish a book.

The butterfly has gone, and the sunshine beckons. It's been a long hard winter in the hills. But the chestnut trees are coming into new leaf, and that's good enough for me. I have never been a fast walker, or a conqueror of mountain peaks, but I can plod along for miles. And that's what I've been doing all my life—plodding along, singing my song, telling my tales in my own unhurried way. I have lived life at my own gentle pace, and if as a result I have failed to get to the top of the mountain (or of anything else), it doesn't matter, the long walk has brought its own sweet rewards; buttercups and butterflies along the way.

Ruskin Bond
Landour, March 2005